Praise for *Fearless Instruction*

"*Fearless Instruction* is a master class in instructional clarity and collaborative professionalism. Grounded in the compelling 90/90/90 research and infused with practical strategies, this book delivers a road map for building schools where high expectations, student voice, and educator efficacy come together to drive deep, sustainable learning. Whether you're a superintendent, school leader, coach, or classroom teacher, you'll find here the tools and inspiration to lead with courage, teach with conviction, and build a culture of excellence that includes every learner."

Dr. Peter Noonan, award-winning superintendent, author, speaker

"*Fearless Instruction* offers a practical but powerful approach to strengthening teaching and learning across a school. The strategies throughout the book are designed to embed effective practices, like checks for understanding, into daily instruction, helping teachers adjust in real time and principals support a culture of responsive teaching. It's a valuable resource for any educator committed to student growth and instructional clarity."

Dr. Beatriz Gonzalez, SBCUSD Director of Family Engagement and District Cluster Lead

"*Fearless Instruction* is an essential text for anyone working in the expansive arenas of education and educational improvement. It is a truly undeniable collection. Each robust chapter provides powerful strategies—including key actions, templates, discussion questions, and more—that teachers, leaders, school-based teams, and district personnel can immediately use to foster and grow cultures of instructional change. Grab your best highlighter! Every page is rich with essential goodness for the bright, fearless road forward!"

Dr. Dru Tomlin, principal, Westerville, Ohio

FEARLESS INSTRUCTION

FEARLESS INSTRUCTION

High-Impact Strategies Inspired
by 90/90/90 Schools

CREATIVE LEADERSHIP SOLUTIONS

Fearless Instruction: High-Impact Strategies Inspired by 90/90/90 Schools
© 2025 Creative Leadership Solutions

All rights reserved. No part of this publication may be reproduced in any form or by any electronic or mechanical means, including information storage and retrieval systems, without permission in writing by the publisher, except by a reviewer who may quote brief passages in a review.

> This book is available at special discounts when purchased in quantity for educational purposes or for use as premiums, promotions, or fundraisers. For inquiries and details, contact the publisher at books@daveburgessconsulting.com.

Published by Creative Leadership Press, a division of Dave Burgess Consulting, Inc.
creativeleadership.net
DaveBurgessConsulting.com

Library of Congress Control Number: 2025942676
Paperback ISBN: 978-1-968898-00-7
Ebook ISBN: 978-1-968898-01-4

Cover and interior design by Liz Schreiter
Produced by Reading List Editorial
ReadingListEditorial.com

ACKNOWLEDGMENTS

In a time when educators are called upon to meet increasingly diverse student needs with precision and purpose, *Fearless Instruction* emerges as an essential guide. This newest publication from Creative Leadership Solutions offers a robust collection of research-based strategies applicable across all grade levels and content areas. Authored by seasoned educational leaders with deep expertise in both theory and practice, it bridges the gap between instructional knowledge and classroom implementation.

What sets *Fearless Instruction* apart is its commitment to practicality. Designed to be immediately usable, it supports collaborative learning teams with data-driven practices and a rich menu of high-yield strategies—empowering educators to make informed, impactful instructional decisions. Whether used in professional learning communities, planning sessions, or classroom coaching, this book provides the tools and insights needed to drive meaningful outcomes for all learners.

My colleagues and I will always be indebted to Creative Leadership Solutions founder Dr. Douglas Reeves, who created the platform in 2015 for this opportunity to exist. Dr. Ann Perez, Director of Professional Learning, fearlessly envisioned the needed resource and led the project to a successful launch.

Of course, *Fearless Instruction* would not exist without the dedication of the many educators who contributed their passion, time, expertise, and unwavering commitment to quality education for all. Special thanks go to Allyson Apsey, Michelle Cleveland, Tony Flach, Emily Freeland, Cedrick Gray, Terry Metzger, Ann Perez, Michelle Picard, Melissa Stephanski, Bill Sternberg, Majalise Tolan, and Melissa Stephanski who shaped this work. Amanda Gomez brought each chapter to life with her graphic design expertise. At the same time, Lisa Fiorilli's thoughtful editing and deep background in K–12 education provided essential clarity and cohesion to this multifaceted project.

May *Fearless Instruction* be the resource that empowers every teacher and leader to be better than they were before. The children are waiting.

Respectfully,
Lisa Almeida
Chief Executive Officer
Creative Leadership Solutions
June 2025

CONTENTS

Foreword 1

Introduction 4

— Section I —
Laying the Foundation: Fostering a Culture of Collaboration

1. Instructional Leadership: Empowering Fearless Instruction 12
   MELISSA STEPHANSKI

2. Collaborative Learning Teams: PLCs Done Right 21
   WILLIAM STERNBERG

3. INFORMative Assessment 31
   MICHELLE CLEVELAND

4. Data-Driven Decision-Making 40
   TONY FLACH

— Section II —
Connecting the Pieces: Putting the 90/90/90 Research to Work

5. The Path to Rigorous Grading 50
   TERRY METZGER

6. Rubrics and Collaborative Scoring: Clear Criteria for Quality Student Work 63
   EMILY FREELAND

7. Nonfiction Writing: Transforming Writing from Fear to Fire 75
   ALLYSON APSEY

8. FAST Feedback Foundations 86
   MAJALISE TOLAN

— Section III —
Finishing the Puzzle: Engaging Everyone

9. Literacy: A Team Sport 96
   MICHELLE PICARD

10. Cross-Disciplinary Integration: More Brains Are Better Than One 109
    ANN MCCARTY PEREZ

11. Open Your Heart, Clear Your Head, Flex Your Hand: Engage Everyone 119
    CEDRICK GRAY

Final Thoughts 129

Endnotes 130

About the Authors 134

FOREWORD

EDUCATORS—THE LEADERS, TEACHERS, COLLEAGUES, AND READERS OF THIS BOOK—NEED INSTRUCTIONAL strategies that are rooted in research and are proven to work with their school, their culture, their schedule, their bargaining agreement, and their budget.

I am often asked, "Which is the best study about…," and the answer is always, "There is no best study." Every study and every research method has its flaws. Our job as educators and school leaders is not to presume to find the best study but rather to synthesize the evidence and come to a rational conclusion.

That has been the life work of Professor John Hattie, who has assembled the world's largest database of educational research.[1] Hattie acknowledges that every study has flaws, but over the course of time, by assembling the data on more than 300 million students, he was able to clearly differentiate the policies and practices that have a greater impact on student learning and those practices and policies that, however popular they may be, have minimal impact.

That is also our work, and, in this book, we present policies and practices that have a greater impact on student learning. Our work is anchored in three qualities that are threaded throughout our instructional practices: evidence, passion, and results.

Evidence alone, even if it comes from a variety of sources and methods, including quantitative methods, qualitative descriptive studies, meta-analyses, and syntheses of meta-analyses, is not enough to create meaningful school change. Passion for teaching and learning, the quality that caused us to become teachers and leaders in the first place, is essential to transform evidence into action.

Evidence

Educational literature is full of hero stories. The problem is that heroism is not a sustainable strategy. Heroism is not easily transmitted from one teacher to the next, and people burn out. Our colleagues have families and other responsibilities. They certainly did not get into education for financial gain, but they also did not agree to a bargain in which the price of success is their physical and mental health.

Therefore, the evidence that is most persuasive is replicable and does not rely upon exceptional resources and unsustainable working conditions. That is the reason that some of the most robust and replicated research findings originated with the 90/90/90 studies—studies of schools with 90% or more of students eligible for free or reduced lunch, 90% or more of students who are ethnic or linguistic minorities, and 90% or more of students who met or exceeded academic standards.[2]

Passion

Even the best evidence-based teaching practices are without value unless the professional educators in the classroom have the bone-deep belief that they make a difference. These teachers know that they can give honest feedback to students because they believe that irrespective of poverty or family conditions, these students can be successful.

In every school I visit, I ask for a show of hands of members of the faculty who are the first generation in their family to go to college. It is not unusual that half the teachers in the room have their hands in the air, proudly waving their success. With this evidence in front of us every day, why would we ever doubt the promising future that our students have?

Students do not always appreciate our challenges in real time, especially if they have been accustomed to low expectations. Passionate educators and leaders love their students, and they love them enough to challenge them, even when it is uncomfortable.

Results

The world of education does not lack research. What we lack is research that teachers in our schools find persuasive and that includes specific practices that work with students. Hattie has a formidable body of research, but he also advocates that teachers "know thy impact" by measuring over a relatively short period of time—four to six weeks—the growth in student achievement that they have caused.[3]

At Creative Leadership Solutions, we engage with educators to display local evidence of impact by having a "Science Fair for Adults." For their presentation, teachers create a simple three-panel display. In the left-hand panel, they identify the challenge—perhaps it's math achievement, reading proficiency, or student behavior (let the teachers choose the challenge that is most important for them). The middle panel is for the professional practice they implemented. Perhaps they moved from homework to in-class practice. Perhaps they changed the way that they engaged with parents. Perhaps they changed their grading practices from the use of the average to evaluating students on how they performed at the time the marking period was completed. The right-hand panel includes their results.

That's it. Three simple panels to visually represent a challenge, the practice, and the results. Display these presentations in the largest gymnasium in the district, and let teachers and administrators draw their own conclusions. We have seen dramatic changes in school districts that have endured years of workshops and lectures without result. When teachers see what really works with their colleagues, their students, and their culture, then change happens quickly, often within a single semester.

Michael Fullan, one of the most influential thinkers and writers in the world of education, used to say that change in schools required five to seven years. When I had dinner with Michael, I said, "You know, whenever people don't want to change, they quote you as saying that change takes five to seven years." He shot back, "That is what I said—35 years ago. I've learned a few things in the meanwhile about accelerating the pace of change." So may it be for all of us—considering the research but then applying our passionate belief in teachers and students and sharing the evidence of what works in our own schools so that change can be swift and sure.

In the following chapters, readers will find specific ideas for effective collaboration for a maximum impact on student achievement. The common element of every chapter is collaboration. The shift, as Dr. Rick DuFour said, was the shift from private practice where each teacher operates independently to public practice where teachers with a deep commitment to equity give the opportunity for every student in every grade level to have consistent expectations, assessments, and academic success.

—Dr. Douglas Reeves, Founder of Creative Leadership Solutions

INTRODUCTION

The Foundation of Fearless Instruction

THE ELEMENTS OF THIS BOOK, *FEARLESS INSTRUCTION*, ARE GROUNDED IN THE ORIGINAL 90/90/90 RESEARCH that Dr. Douglas Reeves conducted. The study focused on identifying the common characteristics and strategies that high poverty, high performing schools implemented to overcome economic and demographic challenges to achieve high academic success. The study is named 90/90/90 to reflect the three defining criteria for the schools:

- More than 90% of the students were from ethnic minority backgrounds.
- More than 90% of the students qualified for free or reduced-price lunches, indicating significant economic challenges.
- More than 90% of the students met or achieved high academic standards, according to independently conducted tests of academic achievement.

Key Findings from the 90/90/90 Study

The study revealed that successful high-poverty, high-minority schools focused on specific adult behaviors and instructional practices:

1 FOCUS ON ACADEMIC ACHIEVEMENT: Schools prioritized academic performance over other goals, with a laser-like focus on student achievement.

2 CLEAR CURRICULUM CHOICES: Schools maintained a rigorous and clearly defined curriculum with an emphasis on reading, writing, and mathematics skills.

3 FREQUENT ASSESSMENT AND FEEDBACK: Regular, data-driven assessments provided multiple opportunities for improvement through regular feedback and allowed teachers to adjust instruction based on student performance.

4 **NONFICTION WRITING:** Nonfiction writing in all subjects, not just English, was a key strategy used to improve overall literacy and critical thinking.

5 **COLLABORATIVE SCORING OF STUDENT WORK:** Schools developed common assessment practices and reinforced them through collaborative scoring and regular exchanges of student work.

A Note from Dr. Reeves

When I first looked at the 90/90/90 data from 135 schools, all with the same per-pupil funding policy and teaching-assignment policies, the typical correlation was evident. High poverty was associated with low student achievement. But what about those schools that, with no extra money or no more extraordinary teachers and leaders, broke the mold? When I visited these exceptional schools and interviewed teachers and leaders, I did not find hidden stores of cash or great benefactors but rather a consistent set of professional practices that were associated with student success. Best of all, these practices were easily replicable by other schools without any change in funding or bargaining agreements. Teachers wanted to be successful—they just needed a clear road map about how to achieve their goals. These practices included nonfiction writing in every subject, collaborative scoring, and a laser-like focus on student achievement. Within a year, the number of 90/90/90 schools in that district tripled and was, ultimately, replicated around the United States.[1]

There were, inevitably, criticisms of these studies. Some critics claimed that documenting success in high-poverty schools results in "blaming the victim"—that is, if high-poverty schools were not successful, it was the fault of the students and teachers. That was certainly not my intent. I believe that students and teachers want to succeed. Teachers devote their lives to a profession that has few rewards. They don't need leaders and policy makers to embrace more initiatives and the latest shiny object—curriculum, technology, and workshops. They just want practical solutions that will help students succeed. The other criticism that emerged in light of these studies was that the standards were too low. That may be legitimate, but when only 21 of 135 schools met the criteria for 90/90/90 recognition, it is fair to say that the accomplishments of these teachers, students, and leaders were exceptional.

Finally, critics of any study of successful high poverty schools claim that the success is based on the work of a few heroic teachers—call it the Jamie Escalante Effect, after the star of the film Stand and Deliver. *But the fact that these practices and the results associated with them have been replicated around the nation suggest that it is not dependent upon a few heroic teachers but rather that these professional practices—not money, not governance structure, and not abrogation of union bargaining agreements—were the causes of student success.*

This is the reason that some of the most robust and replicated research findings originated with the 90/90/90 studies. *Fearless Instruction* is designed to preserve the integrity of the original study while providing timely updates to strategies that can be implemented in any school.

John Hattie and Visible Learning Effect Sizes

Among the many educational researchers influencing schools today, few have had as wide-reaching and lasting an impact as Dr. John Hattie. Dr. Douglas Reeves often notes that it is easy to find research to support nearly any opinion. When shaping our instructional practices, therefore, it is essential to look for a preponderance of evidence. This is one reason Hattie's work has gained such widespread traction: He synthesized findings from over 1200 meta-analyses to identify which factors have the greatest impact on student learning not only in the classroom but also in the school and at home.

A meta-analysis is a research method that combines data from multiple studies on the same topic to identify consistent patterns, trends, and conclusions. An effect size is a numerical value that indicates the level of impact an intervention or variable can have. In *Visible Learning: The Sequel*,[2] Hattie explains that an effect size of 0.4 represents the benchmark for a typical year's growth. Practices with effect sizes over 0.4 are considered high-impact, capable of producing more than a year's growth in a year. Those below 0.4 may actually hinder progress and widen achievement gaps.

Throughout *Fearless Instruction*, readers will find references to Hattie's research and the effect sizes of key instructional strategies. These insights are not just theoretical; they serve as a practical guide for choosing practices that truly accelerate learning to help close learning gaps for all students.

Social-Emotional Learning

The best learning environment is one that supports student success both academically and socially, and we address social-emotional learning specifically in Chapter 10. When students experience success, they become more engaged and more motivated and behavior concerns often fade into the background. This holds true not only for academic learning but also for the development of social and emotional skills. These skills are best understood by applying the five core competencies developed by the Collaborative for Academic, Social, and Emotional Learning (CASEL):

THE CASEL 5				
SELF-AWARENESS	SELF-MANAGEMENT	SOCIAL-AWARENESS	RELATIONSHIP SKILLS	RESPONSIBLE DECISION-MAKING
Develop a healthy sense of who we are	Manage stress and emotions to achieve goals	Understand the views of others, perspective taking, and empathy	Engage effectively with others, build relationships, communicate, and advocate	Make caring and constructive choices

Caldwell Perez (2023) The Successful Middle School Counseling Program

INTRODUCTION

Educators know that students walk into classrooms with a wide range of academic abilities. This book focuses on the strategies that help all students succeed academically, but it is equally important to recognize the variability in students' social and emotional skills, such as managing emotions, demonstrating empathy, communicating effectively, and making good decisions. Just as with reading or math, social-emotional learning must be intentionally embedded into instruction and consistently reinforced across all subject areas and grade levels.

Ask any teenager how they've learned the most about relationships, self-management, or resilience, and you'll likely hear, "The hard way." In reality, what they mean is that they learn best through authentic experiences: real-world opportunities that allow them to navigate challenges, reflect on their identity and social impact, collaborate with others, understand divergent perspectives, and grow. The most powerful social-emotional learning instruction is embedded in the day-to-day life of a classroom and school community.

When academic and social-emotional development are integrated into meaningful, experience-based learning, students gain the tools they need to thrive, not just in school, but in life. These tools, when grounded in the CASEL framework, support students in becoming cognizant citizens, responsible decision-makers, and compassionate peers. Embedding these competencies into the daily lives of students both enriches the school culture and enhances the learning experience.

Power Standards™: Too Many Standards, Too Little Time

Since the start of the standards movement, bitter controversies have divided educators, leaders, and policy makers about standards. However, one issue garners widespread agreement: There are too many standards with too little time to teach them effectively.

Most frameworks, including the well-intentioned Common Core State Standards, assume that students need only one year to master all grade-level content. In practice, many students require significantly more time. Without the luxury of extended school days, educators are forced to make tough choices about what to prioritize—and often do so in isolation.

When every standard is treated as equal, instruction becomes rushed and fragmented and essential skills may be glossed over. That is where Power Standards come in.

At Creative Leadership Solutions, we help educators identify and implement Power Standards, which are the essential skills that form the backbone of the guaranteed and viable curriculum. With Power Standards, schools can focus on teaching deeply rather than broadly.

> "When collaborative teams focus on mastery over coverage, student achievement improves. If teachers are going to make prioritization decisions anyway, it's best done as a team—with shared criteria and clear focus."
>
> —DOUGLAS REEVES[3]

Power Standards are defined by the following:

- **LEVERAGE:** Skills that apply across disciplines.
- **ENDURANCE:** Skills that are required over time.
- **ESSENTIAL:** Skills that are needed for the next grade level or course of instruction.

Why We Are Excited About This Book

We are excited about this book because it brings together a dynamic collection of voices united by a common purpose: to carry forward and evolve the foundational work of the 90/90/90 schools. Grounded in research and rich with practical strategies, this book is for educators who are ready to lead with clarity, collaborate with purpose, and teach with courage.

Each chapter highlights a critical component of building fearless schools, beginning with strong instructional leadership and culminating in a renewed commitment to engaging every learner. From shaping fearless learning environments to developing high-functioning collaborative learning teams and from transforming feedback to empowering student voice through writing, this book delivers a comprehensive toolkit for school teams dedicated to real, sustainable change.

What unites these chapters is their deep alignment to the daily realities of today's schools: realities that are complex, collaborative, and full of potential. Whether you are a building leader, instructional coach, or classroom teacher, you'll find insights, encouragement, and actionable strategies throughout these pages. We're proud to bring together a community of contributors who don't just believe in better schools but are building them every day.

More than a resource, this book is a road map for navigating the intricacies of teaching and learning with fearlessness, integrity, and an unwavering belief in every student's success.

About This Book

Fearless Instruction is organized into three sections, each accompanied by a section summary and reflection questions to support ongoing learning and application.

Section I, Laying the Foundation: Fostering A Culture of Collaboration

This section outlines the necessary structures to facilitate fearless instruction and includes the following key components:

- **Instructional Leadership.** The practice of guiding and supporting teaching and learning to improve student outcomes by school or district leaders.
- **Collaborative Learning Teams.** A highly productive group of individuals who collaborate to positively impact the outcomes of student learning by analyzing learning standards, discussing instructional practices, and determining evidence of student understanding.

- **Data-Driven Decision-Making.** The process of using data to inform and guide instructional decisions that impact teaching and learning.
- **Assessment for Learning.** The ongoing process of using formative assessment methods to gather, interpret, and use evidence of student learning to improve teaching and learning.

Section II, Connecting the Pieces: Putting the 90/90/90 Research to Work

This section outlines key ideas for Tier 1 instruction that when used together provide students with consistent and rigorous experiences. Key components in this section and how we define them are the following:

- **Cognitive Rigor.** The ability to develop flexible and strategic thinking, consider multiple perspectives and approaches, and apply old knowledge and skills in new situations.
- **Teacher Clarity and Collaborative Scoring.** Clear communication of learning intentions, success criteria, and instructional steps to help students understand what they're learning, why it matters, and how to succeed. Additionally, teacher clarity provides consistent expectations so that adults can calibrate their scoring and feedback.
- **Nonfiction Writing.** Writing that students generate in all subjects, not just in language arts, to explain, describe, or reflect on what they are learning.
- **FAST Feedback.** Information about a task that helps to fill the gap between what is understood and what is expected. FAST stands for fair, accurate, specific, and timely.

Section III, Finishing the Puzzle: Engaging Everyone

This section outlines focus areas and strategies that can and should be used in every classroom. Key components in this section and how we define them are these:

- **Focus on Literacy.** The understanding that literacy should be a shared responsibility across all content areas, not just something taught in language arts classes. Literacy is the foundation for success in every subject.
- **Cross-Disciplinary Integration.** The process of two or more subject areas working together to plan crosscutting concepts and skills that can be taught and reinforced in multiple classrooms.
- **Engaging All.** A decision to see the world, the content area, and the subject matter through the eyes of the student by personalizing instruction and engaging every student.

Every chapter explores the **"why," "how," and "what"** of fearless instruction, offering research-backed strategies that you can use individually or combine for greater impact. Every chapter includes a reproducible tool to support thoughtful planning and implementation.

As you move through the book, you'll see how the key structures and strategies connect—like puzzle pieces—to create a cohesive, student-centered framework for quality instruction.

—Creative Leadership Solutions Associates

– SECTION I –
LAYING THE FOUNDATION

Fostering a Culture of Collaboration

INSTRUCTIONAL LEADERSHIP
Empowering Fearless Instruction

BIG IDEAS
CULTURE
STEWARDSHIP
RETENTION
GROWTH
PSYCHOLOGICAL SAFETY

EMPOWERING FEARLESS INSTRUCTION IS THE GUIDING PIECE OF THE PUZZLE, THE ONE that helps align the rest. Instructional leadership brings vision, coherence, and momentum to the work of teaching and learning, ensuring every piece connects with purpose. In this chapter, we highlight the role of instructional leaders in affecting student achievement, and we explore how leaders can improve school culture, support high-quality instruction, and develop staff in meaningful, lasting ways.

Instructional leadership is not solely the responsibility of administrators. Rather, it is a shared responsibility among everyone involved with teaching and learning. In fact, school administrators should see themselves as lead instructional teachers. This mindset fosters a culture for shared ownership of student outcomes. To support this vision, school leaders can take intentional actions to create safe, supportive learning environments and to provide staff with the resources and support they need to thrive.

> "It's not just about potlucks and Sudoku tournaments. My staff knows, when you need me, I'm there."
> —JOHN WEBB, ELEMENTARY PRINCIPAL, MODESTO, CA

Instructional leaders who foster a robust learning culture lay the groundwork for long-term academic success and personal growth for both students and staff. Successful school leaders use their daily interactions with others to nurture the learning culture so that it is psychologically safe, and they prioritize time for leaders and teachers to reflect and collaborate.

When change is necessary, effective building leaders recognize and honor the critical influence of school culture. A successful school culture does not appear by magic or grow overnight. It requires energy and consistency.

This chapter discusses three major responsibilities of the school instructional leader in empowering fearless instruction:

- Nurturing a culture for learning
- Supporting instruction
- Recruiting, retaining, and developing staff

This chapter also provides points of reflection for teachers to exercise their voice in the shared learning environment. The end of the chapter includes a self-assessment designed for leaders to assess their leadership practices and to set goals for guiding others through *Fearless Instruction*. Teachers are encouraged to start their fearless instruction journey by taking the assessment to reflect on current leadership practices.

THE WHY

> "Across six rigorous studies estimating principals' effect using panel data, principals' contributions to student achievement were nearly as large as the average effects of teachers identified in similar studies. Principals' effects, however, are larger in scope because they are averaged over all students in a school, rather than a classroom."
>
> —WALLACE FOUNDATION

The influence of the classroom teacher on student learning is well-documented; however, teachers are not the only ones who have a major influence on student achievement. School leaders who prioritize instruction and professional learning can have an even greater impact on student achievement than any single teacher.[1]

Students and teachers deserve a leader who spends quality time in the classroom, understands the challenges, and actively works to support instruction and student learning. Unfortunately, leaders often struggle to find the time to engage with instructional leadership because they are burdened with management tasks. Fearless instructional leaders are those who see themselves as the lead teacher, with the school as their classroom. This chapter helps those who are in leadership roles evaluate their current priorities and forge the path toward instructional leadership.

THE HOW

Nurturing a Culture for Learning

In *Fearless Schools*,[2] Douglas Reeves reminds us that the key to nurturing a school's culture is to build trust and establish credibility. As educators, we know that the following examples are model environments for student achievement.

- A school campus where trust resides and promises made are promises kept. Where staff feel valued as professionals, students feel safe and cared for, and parents feel encouraged to provide their valuable support.
- A school where hallways breathe with vibrance and energy. Where teachers invest in true collaboration by analyzing data and overcoming challenges with no fear of mistakes.
- Classrooms where high-yield teaching strategies prevail. Where lessons are intentionally crafted to engage all learners and lead each student to true content mastery. Where students are excited and actively engaged in their learning and learners receive multiple opportunities to demonstrate understanding.

Taking Action

The following leadership moves are designed to help leaders think through specific actions to take to nurture their school's learning environment.

LEADERSHIP MOVE #1
Develop a psychologically safe environment for staff and students.

PSYCHOLOGICAL SAFETY is the antidote for a fearful environment. Research shows that fear lowers oxytocin, which limits the ability to learn.[3] Leaders who promote the idea of psychological safety as a health and wellness imperative take specific actions and make decisions in the best interest of their organization.	**HOW TO NURTURE IT** - Make an unwavering commitment to build trusting relationships with staff, students, families, and community. - Normalize mistakes as part of the learning process for everyone. - Take swift action to address any threat to school safety without delay. - Provide a sense of inclusivity, order, and safety for all who enter.

INSTRUCTIONAL LEADERSHIP

LEADERSHIP MOVE #2
Establish nonnegotiable norms for collaboration and high expectations for instructional practices.

COLLABORATION is the act of educators working interdependently to discuss and solve teaching and learning issues and approaches. Collaborative Learning Teams (CLTs) are the best way to nurture collaboration, and leaders who believe in collective efficacy hold themselves, staff, and students to high expectations with the understanding that goals are achieved when a team works together.

HOW TO NURTURE IT

- Stay true to the mission of student achievement, build teamwork, and believe in shared decision-making.
- Understand that team building and trust are critical for sharing ideas, asking for assistance, challenging each other to higher levels, and working in sync each day.
- Set educational goals, leverage high-yield instructional practices, analyze data, provide support for teacher success, and ensure safety for collaboration and vulnerability.

LEADERSHIP MOVE #3
Provide feedback that is FAST (fair, accurate, specific, and timely) to staff to encourage growth.

FAST FEEDBACK is intentional and actionable feedback provided by leaders to coach their teachers into better performance, not evaluate them into it. Every classroom visit is an opportunity to support instruction through feedback, coaching, and reflective discussions.

HOW TO NURTURE IT

- Spend quality time in classrooms to ensure that teachers guide student learning by monitoring progress, analyzing data, and providing FAST feedback.
- Inspect what you expect, accept that making mistakes can lead to learning, provide support for the efforts, and celebrate the successes.
- Maintain confidentiality and provide support for all areas of need in teacher development.

REFLECTION

Leaders, reflect on your current instructional leadership style and how you might grow as a leader and support teachers' development. Teachers, reflect on the leaders in your building and the ways they support your instructional practice and growth.

Supporting Instruction

Leaders who empower fearless instruction actively support instruction by thoughtfully allocating resources and removing barriers to student achievement.

Promoting Resource Stewardship

Instructional leaders should allocate resources in a way that aligns with the school's vision, goals, priorities, and contextual needs. For example, if research-based curriculum, ample teacher materials, and robust professional learning are priorities, then the school budget should align with those priorities and allocate funds accordingly. A good practice for school leaders is to analyze the school budget to determine if their school's priorities and vision are easily discernable.

School leaders are also charged with effectively allocating the limited resource of time. Just as with the budget, school leaders should design master schedules to reflect the school's priorities. Schedules must not only provide adequate time for instruction and learning of subject-area content but also authentic assessments, extension or remediation opportunities, student choice, physical wellness, and the arts. If these priorities are important to student achievement, then the schedule should include adequate time to ensure they happen. Fearless instructional leaders understand that allocating resources, particularly money and time, is about comprehensively aligning all available resources to support the learning needs of all students.

> **REFLECTION**
>
> Leaders, reflect on how you design the budget and allocate time to support all learners, including staff. Teachers, reflect on how your instructional practice is impacted or supported by the budget and the schedule.

Removing Barriers

Instructional leaders also need to identify and remove barriers to student achievement by addressing them in a straightforward, progressive manner.

Strategies to address barriers:

- Review a school's systems, routines, and processes for effectiveness.
- Consistently analyze student data to determine gains and losses. Use the analysis to question which barriers impede progress, and then appropriately address them.
- Examine special education needs, language needs, physical needs, emotional needs, and behavioral needs and support with resources that remove or bypass barriers.

> **REFLECTION**
>
> Leaders, reflect on the types of barriers you see in your building and what systems you have in place to address them. Teachers, reflect on the barriers you see in your classroom and the ways that leaders can support you with resources.

Recruiting, Retaining, and Developing Staff

The most important resource in schools is our staff. Period. The staff provides the heartbeat of the school. They shape the school's culture, care for students' physical and mental wellness, lead critical learning, and build bridges with families and the community.

One of the most crucial responsibilities of school leadership is hiring and retaining high-quality educators. Leaders start by developing an intentional process to hire staff with a passion for student learning and a yearning for continual professional growth. Once staff is hired, leaders must provide a psychologically safe work environment grounded in strong relationships, support, and opportunities to grow. When leaders listen, understand mistakes, address concerns, keep promises, and provide support, they create a work environment favorable for attracting and retaining the best educators.[4]

> "Teachers are some of the best of us. We unite around the core principle that we all could be somewhere else, doing something else, and making more money, but we get up every morning and show up. Regardless of what lies ahead, we show up, as simple as it sounds, to be the support system our students need."
>
> —JONATHAN WILLIAMS, HIGH SCHOOL PRINCIPAL, EDMONSON COUNTY, KY

PRO TIP

Involve teachers or teacher teams in your interview process. This practice provides a professional leadership opportunity and helps provide diverse viewpoints on potential candidates.

In addition to recruiting and retaining staff, instructional leaders create and provide time for relevant professional development. Leaders know that a teacher's capabilities unlock the potential for learning in their classrooms. One way to unlock that potential is through high-quality, ongoing professional learning that includes collaborative learning teams. As highlighted by the National Staff Development Council, teacher collaboration is a means of working "smarter and better."[5] (See Chapter 2 for more on Collaborative Learning Teams.)

Because fearless leaders understand the importance of teachers learning from each other, they not only embed time in the schedule for teams to meet but also ensure that the allotted time is utilized correctly. When leaders harness the strength of collaborative learning teams (CLTs), they unleash the power of collective efficacy, which is proven to be one of the highest effect sizes in the classroom.[6] (See the introduction for more about John Hattie and effect sizes.)

REFLECTION

Leaders, reflect on how you recruit, retain, and develop staff. What routines are working? Where do you see areas for improvement? Teachers, reflect on how leaders in your school nurture your growth and development. What strategies work for you? Where do you see areas for improvement?

Instructional leadership impacts every stakeholder and provides a critical linchpin for the success of all. The responsibility is tremendous, but when school leaders accept the role of instructional leader, the school community achieves great gains.

> **What Fearless Instructional Leaders Do:**
> - Encourage risk taking, innovation, and creativity.[7]
> - Celebrate teachers as they increase their capacity, try new teaching approaches, ask questions, and collaborate to help each other be better.
> - Plan for intentional data-based training.
> - Implement faculty meeting learning sessions.
> - Schedule time for peer collaboration.
> - Embed growth opportunities such as coaching, mentoring, peer classroom visits, and relevant book studies throughout the school year.
> - Provide the resources and development teachers need.

THE WHAT

Leaders, start your *Fearless Instruction* journey by taking this self-assessment. After you have completed the book, take the self-assessment again to provide data for your own growth as an instructional leader and for leading others through the process.

Teachers, start your *Fearless Instruction* journey by taking this assessment as an evaluation of current leadership practices in your school. After you have completed the book, you may want to revisit this assessment to reflect on the types of support you need most or areas where your school leaders can improve.

ACTION STEPS

- ❑ Intentionally shape a psychologically safe environment where curiosity, collaboration, and high expectations thrive for both students and staff.
- ❑ Identify and eliminate barriers that hinder teaching and learning. Align time, tools, and support to what matters most.
- ❑ Prioritize recruiting, retaining, and growing staff through meaningful feedback, professional development, and leadership opportunities.
- ❑ Use the Fearless Instruction Leadership Self-Assessment to identify growth areas and to commit to actionable next steps. Fearless Instruction starts with you.

Fearless Instruction Leadership Self-Assessment

1 – Not yet   **2** – I am doing okay   **3** – I am a pro

Nurturing a Culture for Learning

Keep the school's vision and mission front and center for staff, students, and visitors.	1	2	3
Be visible in classrooms, hallways, and shared spaces.	1	2	3
Build strong relationships with students, staff, and caretakers personally.	1	2	3
Normalize mistakes and model accountability when you make your own.	1	2	3
Visit classrooms daily and give meaningful, actionable feedback.	1	2	3
Communicate clearly, consistently, and with transparency.	1	2	3
Set clear expectations for collaboration across grade levels and departments.	1	2	3
Solve problems proactively and follow up with timely communication.	1	2	3
Build trust by following through (promises made, promises kept).	1	2	3
Model lifelong learning by actively participating in professional development.	1	2	3
Support high-functioning Collaborative Learning Teams (CLTs) across the school.	1	2	3

Promoting Resource Stewardship and Removing Barriers to Support Instruction

Use surveys and committees to gather staff input on policies and school practices.	1	2	3
Include staff in conversations about budgeting and resource needs.	1	2	3
Ask for feedback to build schedules that support instruction and wellness.	1	2	3

2025 Creative Leadership Press. This page may be reproduced for classroom use only. All other rights reserved.

Fearless Instruction Leadership Self-Assessment (Continued)

Form inclusive, unbiased committees to examine routines and systems in the school.	1	2	3
Use data to identify learning barriers and to request resources to remove them.	1	2	3

Recruiting, Retaining, and Developing Staff

Offer coaching and mentoring, especially for new or early-career teachers.	1	2	3
Turn faculty meetings into learning opportunities, including book studies led by staff.	1	2	3
Celebrate and recognize professional growth, effort, and excellence.	1	2	3
Foster a positive work culture that makes people want to join and stay.	1	2	3
Use intentional hiring practices (e.g., committees, demo lessons, reference checks).	1	2	3

Leaders, reflect on how you will support your teachers.

Teachers, reflect on what you might need from your leader to be successful.

BIG IDEAS
COLLABORATION
COLLECTIVE EFFICACY
NORMS
FEEDBACK LOOP

COLLABORATIVE LEARNING TEAMS
PLCs Done Right

THIS CHAPTER REPRESENTS A CONNECTING PUZZLE PIECE—COLLABORATIVE LEARNING Teams (CLTs) link all the other pieces together, aligning purpose, practice, and progress toward a shared vision for student success. In this chapter, we outline the purpose and actions of CLTs and the impact they can have on student achievement such as

- analyzing learning standards,
- planning effective instruction,
- identifying evidence of student learning,
- discussing data collaboratively,
- developing common assessments, and
- designing action plans for intervention and extension.

This chapter also includes a six-step process for setting up and strengthening CLTs.

The value of the collaborative process is well established in research. In their work, Shand and Goddard studied the initial impact of collaboration and its growth over time, and their research shows that stronger collaboration leads to growth in differentiated instruction, student focus, collective efficacy, and trust. They found that high-functioning collaborative teams are "positive predictors of change in teacher practice, instructional climate, and trust relations."[1] CLTs provide a win-win—they positively impact student achievement, and they increase teacher effectiveness and job satisfaction.

Collaborative Learning Teams are at the heart of effective professional learning communities, though the depth of their implementation can vary from school to school. In some schools, the CLT process is still emerging. Teachers may meet to discuss some aspects of planning, logistics, duty schedules, or events but may not yet fully embrace the shift from a focus on teaching to a focus on learning.

When CLTs commit to the full collaborative process of discussing standards, planning assessments, examining data, designing Tier 1 instruction, and adjusting to meet student needs, they move beyond what Dufour and Reeves call "PLC Lite."[2] Moving beyond this is where the true potential to transform outcomes for both students and educators begins.

Because schools are ever-changing landscapes with new initiatives, curriculum adoptions, shifting leadership priorities, and high teacher turnover, CLTs can easily lose focus. However, CLTs offer the perfect structure to face these challenges head on and support the effective implementation of any initiative. When CLTs maintain focus on student achievement and growth, they can quickly realign their practice to regain momentum.

THE CLT GOAL: Improve student outcomes.

THE CLT PROCESS: Use data to support collaborative work that focuses on standards, instruction, assessment, and differentiation.

The end of this chapter includes an easy process and template for CLTs to implement a feedback loop and guide conversations.

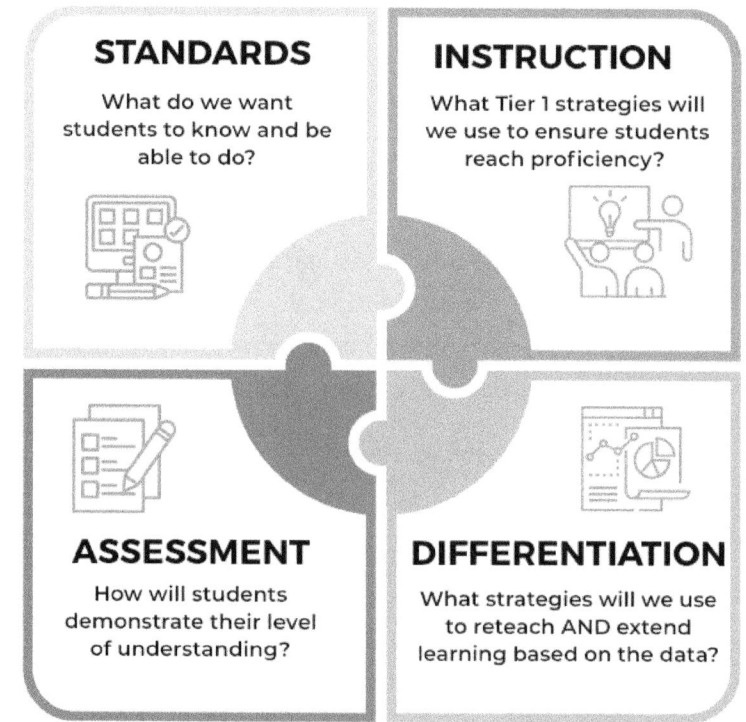

THE WHY

Teaching is complex, and the list of responsibilities can feel endless. But when educators come together through collaboration, they gain strength, clarity, and a shared purpose. Collaborative Learning Teams provide a unified, intentional structure that helps focus their work on four key areas: **standards, assessment, instruction, and differentiation.** The power of CLTs lies not just in shared work, but in shared growth.

Effective implementation of CLTs is one of the most promising strategies for developing the capacity of school staff to assume collective responsibility for improving student and adult learning.[3] According to Hattie's research, collective efficacy has one of the highest positive effect sizes (1.34), demonstrating the power of the collaborative team. (See the introduction for more on effect sizes.) When established with clear guidelines and effective feedback, CLTs become a decision-making body, allowing for true shared leadership opportunities.

- Through the work of CLTs, teachers foster trust, embrace vulnerability, and learn to lean on one another in supporting best practice approaches to better impact student results.
- When a team of individuals believes that, through their unified efforts, they can overcome challenges and produce the intended outcomes, groups are more effective.[4]
- Decisions about the instructional program are no longer solely the responsibility of the school leader. Instead, these decisions now rest with the collective whole of the building, allowing the entire team to more accurately identify and respond to the actual needs of students through consistent analysis of their work.

Not only do effective CLTs positively impact student learning, but they also provide teachers with the benefit of additional time:

- Teachers gain time because they are no longer planning, assessing, and reflecting in isolation.
- Teachers gain time because they are collaboratively implementing and evaluating focused lessons that use data and evidence in student work.
- Teachers spend less time after school or on the weekends planning, grading, or thinking of ideas for their next unit of instruction.

It can be easy to lose focus on consistent support of collaborative teams, so the conditions for successful structures must first be crafted. The following steps provide a path to success, both in establishing collaborative learning teams and in enhancing professional practices within existing teams.

THE HOW

Step 1: Establish a Shared "Why" for Tier 1 Consistency

When implementing a new strategy, initiative, or program, it's essential to begin by clarifying the "why" behind the practice. Just as students better engage when they understand the purpose of their learning, adult learners are more likely to commit when the rationale is clear and relevant.

In the case of Collaborative Learning Teams, the primary "why" is to build consistency in Tier 1 instruction so that every student has access to high-quality learning experiences regardless of who their teacher is.

To surface the current reality and spark discussion within your CLT, start with the following reflective questions. Each team member should respond using a tool that allows them to submit answers anonymously, displaying collective results in real time. This could include digital tools as well as analog options like sticky notes on a poster, colored cards, or dot voting. After they rate their confidence as Very Confident, Somewhat Confident, Not Sure, or Not Confident, the team can reflect on shared perceptions and areas for growth.

1. How confident are we that at least 80% of our teaching staff are teaching and assessing their learning standards at the intended level of rigor?
2. How confident are we that at least 80% of our CLT teams have calibrated expectations for proficient student performance on class tasks, assignments, and assessments?

Real-time polling results often reveal gaps in confidence—typically clustering around the Somewhat Confident or Not Sure rating—and seeing this data helps teams confront the need for consistency and provides a compelling, shared reason to invest in effective CLT work.

The consistency with both expectations and instruction created through CLTs is the foundation of collective teacher efficacy. By anchoring the work in a shared "why," teams can return to this purpose again and again to stay focused and united.

> **PRO TIP**
> If your team needs to add additional norms, keep them grounded in the CLT process and in enhancing instructional practices.

Step 2: Establish Norms for Meetings

Establishing norms in CLTs sets a strong foundation for focus, collaboration, and respectful engagement among team members. Norms are shared agreements about how a group will work together. When intentionally developed, they support equitable participation, creating space for team members to bring their full, authentic selves to the team's work.[5]

Sample norms for high performing CLTs:

- Meetings begin and end on time.
- All members have equal voices.
- The team remains focused on solutions.
- All members arrive prepared for the meeting.
- The team grounds statements in evidence (either from student evidence of understanding or other data).
- All members are present and actively participate in the conversation.

There are a number of ways to create building-wide norms, but the following steps provide an easy way to reach consensus.

Guiding moves for establishing team norms:

- **GATHER INITIAL INPUT FROM TEAMS:** Choose a digital or face-to-face approach based on your school's culture and communication style, and invite each team to identify their own working norms.
- **DEVELOP SHARED NORMS THROUGH TEAM INPUT:** Collect team-generated norms, identify common themes, and build consensus around a set of building-wide norms. In some schools, each team may develop their own norms if needed.
- **COMMUNICATE AND REINFORCE THE NORMS:** Share the agreed-upon norms with staff, and revisit them regularly to ensure they guide daily practice.

The process of getting to building-wide norms is adaptable, but the goal of consistent norms for all CLTs remains concrete.

Step 3: Empower Every Voice Through Purposeful Roles

To ensure that CLT meetings are focused, productive, and inclusive, team members should take on defined roles. These roles are more than logistical; they are essential to creating shared ownership, building trust, and ensuring that every voice contributes to the collective work of improving instruction.

Importantly, the facilitator role is most effective when held by a peer, as this reinforces shared ownership and trust among team members. However, in the early stages, especially when teams are newly formed or still building collaborative momentum, it can be helpful for a leader, coach, or administrator to temporarily serve as the facilitator. This kind of support can model effective team practices and help establish strong norms. Once the team is functioning confidently and consistently, the facilitator role can transition to a peer to truly foster a culture of collective leadership.

The following core roles are considered nonnegotiable for every CLT:

- **FACILITATOR:** Guides the meeting, enforces norms, and ensures equity of voice.
- **TIMEKEEPER:** Keeps the group on pace so conversations stay focused and outcomes are reached.
- **RECORDER:** Captures key ideas, decisions, and next steps; ensures documentation is shared.

In addition to these essential roles, consider adding roles that enhance and elevate the quality of team dialogue:

- **PERSPECTIVE PARTNER:** Offers alternative viewpoints or questions assumptions to help the team think critically and avoid groupthink.
- **CLARIFIER:** Summarizes agreements and ensures next steps are clearly articulated before the meeting ends.

Step 4: Identify the Structure of the CLT Meeting

CLT meetings should address four critical areas by answering specific, guiding questions. The key is pacing. Teams do not need to cover all four focus areas in one meeting, but revisiting each regularly and intentionally helps keep the work focused, manageable, and aligned to student needs.

- **STANDARDS:** What do we want students to know and be able to do?
- **ASSESSMENT:** How will students demonstrate their level of understanding?
- **INSTRUCTION:** What Tier 1 strategies will we use to ensure students reach proficiency?
- **DIFFERENTIATION:** How will we reteach or extend based on the data?

> **PRO TIP**
>
> Rotate roles regularly to build leadership skills across the team and keep every member actively engaged in the process. This is especially important if there are more team members than roles.

Step 5: Schedule Time for CLTs

If collaboration is truly a priority, it must be reflected in how we allocate our most valuable resource: time. Regularly scheduled CLT meetings, ideally 45 to 60 minutes each week, create the consistent space teams need to analyze student learning, align instruction, and make meaningful progress. Without dedicated time, even the most well-intentioned efforts stall.

Schools can carve out this time by using existing planning periods or windows of time before or after school or by creatively restructuring schedules to protect and prioritize collaboration.

Step 6: Create a Feedback Loop

Because it is impossible for building principals, assistant principals, instructional coaches, and special service providers to attend CLT meetings every time they meet, a feedback loop to document discussions is vital to success. Instead of creating and filling out forms just to check a box, build a simple feedback loop that helps leaders give support on a regular basis. The feedback loop is not designed as a "gotcha" opportunity to identify team missteps. Rather, it is an opportunity to provide authentic, actionable feedback to support the process.

If using a form to document the CLT's work, the Recorder completes the form and submits it to a shared drive or folder within an established deadline (e.g., directly after the meeting or within 24 hours of the meeting). If using an email, the Recorder follows the same established deadline. Once submitted, the leadership team should establish a routine of reviewing these notes and providing feedback on a timely basis. This feedback loop should run consistently and smoothly throughout the school year.

CLTs can use a form to document their work, or, as Douglas Reeves suggests,[6] write a concise "four-line email" for teams to report on Standards, Assessment, Instruction, and Differentiation.

> **PRO TIP**
>
> Be thoughtful when adding extra requirements or information. Too much can unintentionally shift the team's focus from meaningful collaboration to mere compliance.

Suggested guidelines for the four-line email:

- **STANDARDS:** Focus on one to three key standards, word for word.
- **ASSESSMENT:** Identify how students will demonstrate their level of understanding.
- **INSTRUCTION:** Identify two to three Tier 1 strategies teachers will use to help students reach proficiency.
- **DIFFERENTIATION:** Identify two to three strategies that teachers will use to reteach and extend based on the data.

THE WHAT

The previous section outlined key steps to set up CLTs for success. Now it's time to bring that foundation to life. This section provides an actionable, student-centered template that Collaborative Learning Teams can use to guide their weekly meetings with purpose and clarity.

The first focus area, **Standards**, gives CLTs an opportunity to align their expectations for student performance by taking a close look at the learning standard the team has identified. Establishing clear outcomes across the team ensures everyone is working toward the same goals. CLTs begin by answering the foundational question: **"What do we want students to know and be able to do?"**

The second focus area, **Assessment**, is when the CLT identifies or creates a uniform method to assess student understanding of the learning standard. The team gathers evidence from the data and discusses it in an apples-to-apples comparison. (See Chapter 3 for more about informative assessment and Chapter 4 for data discussions.) To ensure that all students have an equal opportunity to demonstrate their understanding, teams need to be consistent in the administration of assessments. The team answers the question **"How will students demonstrate their level of understanding?"**

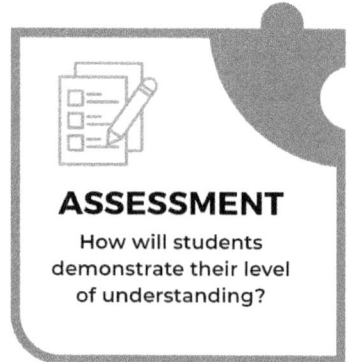

Align **Assessment** practices. Sometimes, the same formative assessment is given in different ways, leading to unfair comparisons. For example, if one teacher reads a science test aloud while another has students read it independently, one is assessing listening and one is assessing reading comprehension, two very different skills. To ensure CLTs analyze data accurately and fairly, assessments must be administered consistently across classrooms.

The third focus area, **Instruction**, is an opportunity for CLTs to identify and share the Tier 1 instructional strategies that are most effective in helping students meet learning goals. When teachers bring their best practices to the table, strategies that truly engage students and lead to results, the entire team benefits and so do all students.

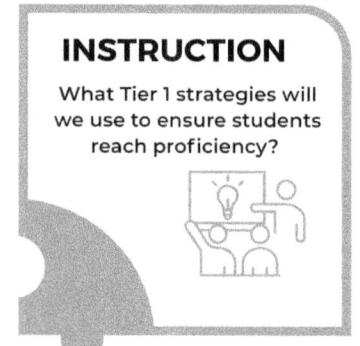

This focus also includes intentional planning for both intervention and extension. Too often, schools lean heavily in one direction based on their student population, but CLTs must design instruction for students who need extra support and challenge those who are ready to go deeper. Prioritizing both ensures that every student is learning, growing, and being pushed to their potential. Together, the team answers the question, **"What Tier 1 strategies will we use to ensure all students reach proficiency?"**

The fourth focus area, **Differentiation**, is when the CLT reviews the determined criteria for proficiency with the data from assessments. The CLT makes plans to 1) address next steps for students who have not demonstrated mastery and 2) determine how to provide extended learning opportunities. To ensure that the needs of all students are met, CLTs must spend an equal amount of time answering the question, **"What strategies will teachers use to reteach AND extend based on the data?"**

The collaborative team process is not a checklist to complete in one sitting; it's an ongoing, intentional cycle in which teams continuously engage with the four focus areas: **Standards**, **Assessment**, **Instruction**, and **Differentiation**.

Do all four areas need to be addressed in a single meeting? Not necessarily. The key is pacing. High-functioning teams prioritize efficiency, returning to each focus area regularly and purposefully. The goal is to engage with all four tenets regularly and systematically, ensuring the work is meaningful, manageable, and aligned to student needs.

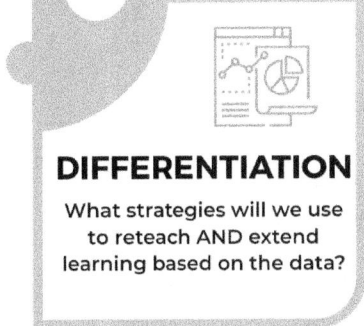

DIFFERENTIATION
What strategies will we use to reteach AND extend learning based on the data?

Create the Action Plan

The last part of the CLT cycle is to create an action plan that summarizes the conversation and outlines steps for the next meeting. The team then closes the feedback loop (see Step 6 in the previous section) by recording the information from the meeting to share with others.

> **PRO TIP**
> Spend the last 5 minutes of your meeting creating the action plan.

Sample action plan items:

- Assign assessment parts to CLT members to build and then share.
- Create logistics, including a timeline, for intervention groups.
- Plan for resources to gather, share, or organize with the team.
- Administer the common assessment and analyze results.

=== **ACTION STEPS** ===

- ❏ Personalize your "why."
- ❏ Establish norms.
- ❏ Assign roles to empower team members.
- ❏ Create time in the schedule for Collaborative Learning Teams.
- ❏ Ensure that a method for creating a feedback loop is established.
- ❏ Implement a complete process to keep the focus on student learning.

Collaborative Learning Teams

Team: _____

Roles:
- Facilitator: _____
- Timekeeper: _____
- Recorder: _____

CLT Goals:

Norms:
- _____
- _____
- _____
- _____
- _____

Team Notes

Date: _____ **Members:** _____

Focus Area	Summary of Discussion
Standards What do we want students to know and be able to do?	
Assessment How will students demonstrate their level of understanding?	
Instruction What Tier 1 strategies will we use to ensure students reach proficiency?	
Differentiation What strategies will we use to reteach AND extend learning based on the data?	
Team Action Plan:	

BIG IDEAS
CHECKS FOR UNDERSTANDING
PRE-ASSESSMENT
PLANNING
SUCCESS CRITERIA

INFORMATIVE ASSESSMENT

THINK OF THIS CHAPTER AS A LINKING PIECE, SMALL BUT POWERFUL IN CONNECTING what students know to what they need next. In this chapter, we'll explore how Collaborative Learning Teams (CLTs) can strengthen instructional practice through an intentional focus on embedded formative assessment. We will examine ways CLTs can plan for both teacher and student actions across all phases of learning and how meaningful assessment data can be collected and used to inform and guide instructional decisions.

> "It if is not going to inform tomorrow's instruction, it's not formative assessment."
>
> —DOUGLAS REEVES

Fearless schools and classrooms are vibrant places of learning supported by the efforts of collaborative learning teams. In high-functioning CLTs, teachers engage in structured conversations about teaching and learning to intentionally shift their instructional practices and planning for student learning.[1]

A key focus for CLTs is the use of assessment for learning. Members work collaboratively to determine what students should know and be able to do, how to best teach the standards, and how to assess students. Reeves reminds us that collaboration between both principals and teachers within the collaborative team is critical for the entire school community to embrace learning.[2]

An Assessment Success Story

At my previous school, when we began the turnaround process, we had a year where we experienced tremendous turnover in staff and started over with nearly 25 new teachers. As we visited classrooms in the first few weeks, we noticed that instructional design, in particular, formative assessment, was not being used for learning. During one of our first staff professional learnings, we asked teachers to bring a printed copy of an upcoming lesson plan. We handed them four highlighters. One color for direct instruction, one color for guided instruction, one color for independent practice, and one color for checking for understanding practices.

Once teachers had highlighted their own lesson plans, we asked them a set of guiding questions as collaborative teams that asked them to think about what their lessons looked and felt like to them and to their students. From this, each team developed their first "Double Plans" with embedded formative assessments tied to success criteria and learning objectives. Over the course of the year, we continued to come back to this level of instructional planning with a focus on using the data. At the end of our third year of work together, the school had achieved 130 points in growth on the California accountability system at the time, and most importantly, the dynamic student learning and joy in the classrooms was evident each day in every class.

The end of this chapter includes an instructional planning tool for embedding formative assessment into your daily lessons.

THE WHY

To cultivate fearless classrooms, CLTs should design the core instructional program to include regular, uncomplicated, and embedded formative assessments as part of every instructional segment during the day. The most impactful formative assessments are designed to be a continuous and integrated process in daily instruction, to continually monitor student progress so that educators can shift and adapt in the moment, and to allow educators to have systems of data collection that are part of their daily routines with students.

> **The benefits of embedded formative assessments:**
>
> - Consistent use of research-based, effective strategies that are integrated into the instructional routine.
> - The opportunity for educators to predict outcomes and students to demonstrate knowledge and skills during learning.[3]

Informative assessment routines do not need to be complex or cumbersome in implementation. Instead, CLTs need to develop simple, effective methods that work with students and allow for teachers to adjust instruction in the moment for student learning. Rick Stiggins wrote, "When it comes to effective assessment, purpose is everything."[4] What the authors of this book have learned from working with teacher teams over many years is that this sentiment continues to be the most important for student learning in classrooms.

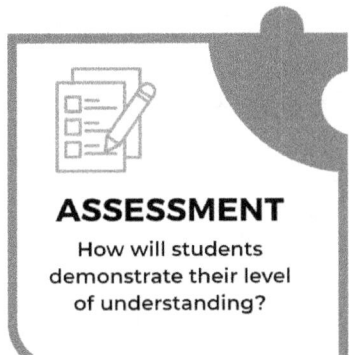

So how do we use CLT conversations to embed good assessment routines? We rely on the tried-and-true tools that we know best. We plan our lessons around both teacher and student actions with instructional routines that are simple, allow for adaptation in the moment, and help both students and teachers track their learning.

THE HOW

Actions for Embedding Formative Assessment

There are five instructional planning actions that CLTs can take together to embed formative assessment into learning. These actions help teams identify student performance and progress based on a Power Standard™ and provide evidence of student knowledge and skills to guide learning. This is the data that will drive the most successful CLT conversations. (See Chapter 4 for the data discussion process.) As we move through this chapter, readers will gain perspective about how to integrate strategies, creating opportunities for ongoing assessment throughout the learning.

INSTRUCTIONAL PLANNING FOR FORMATIVE ASSESSMENT

1. Identify the standard, learning intentions, and success criteria for the lesson.

2. Explicitly describe teacher and student actions during the lesson. Plan for direct, guided, and independent learning tasks.

3. Use a pre-assessment that is based on the success criteria.

4. Identify specific checks for understanding and strategies within the learning tasks.

5. Use exit assessment tied back to the success criteria.

Identify the Standard, Learning Intentions, and Success Criteria

As CLTs begin planning, it is critical to identify learning intentions. For the purposes of this chapter, when we discuss a lesson, we are referring to a single learning period. As teachers meet in CLTs, they should identify learning intentions and success criteria based on the standard(s) they are teaching. Success criteria should be measurable and attainable during the time allotted for the lesson. Using success criteria in the lesson helps both the student and the teacher know exactly what is expected so that each can monitor the learning as they move through the lesson. (See Chapter 7 for more on success criteria.)

Explicitly Describe Teacher and Student Actions

An effective method for developing a period of instruction is for the teacher or CLT to use a template to document their thinking. The most productive and helpful templates are built to outline both teacher and student actions throughout the learning process.

A simple T-chart can be a simple yet effective tool to use as teams collaborate. The deliberate conversation about what it looks like to be both a teacher and student in the classroom is very powerful when working to identify opportunities for checking for understanding. To carefully plan for teacher and student actions, include the following:

- Direct instruction for new content
- Teacher-guided activities that include peer discussion and checks for understanding
- Individual reflection time
- Lesson closure

> **PRO TIP**
>
> Link resources including exemplars, questions, text excerpts, outside resources, and graphic organizers so that all team members and, in some cases, students can access and use the plan throughout instruction.

Use a Pre-Assessment

Once the success criteria are determined, the CLT can choose the best pre-assessment tool to use to start the lesson. This tool should be simple and brief, and it should provide the teacher with immediate feedback about student progress from the previous lesson. Pre-assessment is a critical component of embedded formative assessment because it lets the teacher and students know where they are starting at the beginning of that instructional period.

Examples of simple pre-assessment tools:

- Quick writes
- 1 to 2 multiple choice questions
- Digital polls
- Self-rating scales
- 4-corners voting
- Agree/disagree statements

Whatever tool the CLT chooses, the pre-assessment is meant to be short and informative and a bridge to the new learning for that instructional period. To avoid cumbersome or time-consuming pre-assessments, CLTs should collaborate to align the pre-assessment tool to the success criteria for the lesson. A pre-assessment is a tool that provides another check to ensure that the success criteria are manageable for the learning time allotted.

Check for Understanding

As students and teachers move beyond the pre-assessment and into the lesson, checking for understanding activates the next level of embedded formative assessment. These instructional routines should be designed to give both the teacher and the student information about the learning and should be implemented at specific points throughout a lesson.

Ways to best execute checking for understanding during a learning period:

- Frequently throughout direct instruction segments
- During guided instructional segments
- At the end of independent learning tasks

Checking for understanding creates the conditions for students to reflect on and share about their learning with each other and the teacher. Feedback from peers and the teacher can extend ideas and help contribute to more active student engagement in the classroom. Because tools for checking for understanding should be an integrated part of the planned lesson, be sure to select one that matches the success criteria and the needs of the lesson.

Assess at the End of Learning

Exit tickets, the final evidence of student learning, are an opportunity for students to "exit" learning at the end of the instructional segment. Exit tickets are one of the most crucial embedded formative assessment tools because both teachers and students must look back to the success criteria and think about how they have met those criteria.

> **PRO TIP**
>
> Collaborative learning teams should select 4 to 5 Tier 1 practices to frequently use as instructional routines to help teachers and students develop skills and efficiency in the tool. Most importantly, these tools allow teachers to collect evidence of student learning to drive instructional decisions.

Quick and easy exit ticket ideas:

- Quick write
- Poll
- Multiple-choice response
- Verbal shares of learning

To assess at the end of learning, teachers should use a tool that requires students to synthesize their learning and share it with the teacher and, if time allows, a peer. For all teachers, these exit tickets guide them to assess where to go next with the unit of learning. For secondary teachers in particular, this strategy may also help them adjust for other student groups that they see after the initial delivery of the instruction.

> **PRO TIP**
>
> For exit tickets, leave 5 minutes after completion to address any immediate errors that could help students enter learning the next time with more knowledge. Complete a quick error analysis with students to remediate miscues before they become habits for learners.

Effective exit tickets:

- Are simple and efficient if used daily
- Become part of the instructional routine
- Are expected and engaged with by students

INFORMATIVE ASSESSMENT

THE WHAT

The following are effective tools that provide evidence of student learning. Many of these tools can be integrated with one another during instructional time.

HOW IT'S DONE	WHAT IT DOES
FORMATIVE STRATEGY: RANDOM SELECTION	
• Call on students randomly. • Use equity sticks or randomized selection tools. • Plan to call on students who will help start or move a conversation. • Plan to give all learners a voice.	• Assesses engagement with and progress toward mastery of content. • Allows for modifications and accommodations, such as prepping a student before they share. • Can be used with direct, guided, and independent instruction.
FORMATIVE STRATEGY: WHITEBOARDS	
• Provide students with a small whiteboard or other type of temporary sharing platform. • Prompt students with short-answer response questions or math problems. • Have students hold up whiteboards to share their learning. • Circulate to observe responses.	• Assesses short phrases or simple problems. • Allows the teacher to develop systems that show evidence of student learning and engagement throughout the lesson. • Can be used for guided or independent practice.
FORMATIVE STRATEGY: TURN, TALK, AND SHARE BACK	
• Develop a question for a short response. • Give students a set amount of time to turn to a peer partner and respond to the question. • Have students share their responses.	• Assesses engagement during direct instruction. • Creates a layer of accountability if cold calling is integrated into the share aspect. • Allows for the teacher to assess student mastery of content prior to moving into more content.

FEARLESS INSTRUCTION

FORMATIVE STRATEGY: THINK–WRITE–PAIR–SHARE	
• Develop a question that requires students to reflect on learning that has just occurred. • Give students time to think and respond in writing. • Have students share their learning with a peer partner. • Facilitate a class conversation about what was shared in peer conversations. • Use sentence frames to collect evidence of learning through writing, listening, and speaking.	• Assesses the knowledge of individual students as well as their ability to articulate learning with a partner. • Creates opportunities for peers to provide feedback to one another and the whole group. • Can be used to assess students individually, in small groups, or as a class.
FORMATIVE STRATEGY: DIGITAL TOOLS	
• Use as part of Think–Write–Pair–Share. • Determine which section of the lesson is best suited to a transition to student devices.	• Provides real-time feedback and error analysis. • Provides evidence of learning that can be shared with CLT teams and students. • Can be used for guided or independent instruction.

ACTION STEPS

- ❑ Engage in ongoing professional learning around formative assessment, data analysis, and effective collaboration.
- ❑ Frame formative assessment as a tool for learning, not just measurement, in all CLT conversations.
- ❑ Use a CLT process that focuses on clear success criteria and frequently assess those criteria.
- ❑ Use a variety of formative assessment tools to monitor student learning throughout the entire learning period.

INSTRUCTIONAL PLANNING FOR FORMATIVE ASSESSMENT

Use this resource with your team as a guide when planning for formative assessment.

1. **Identify the Standard, Learning Intentions, and Success Criteria**

2. **Explicitly Describe Teacher and Student Actions**

3. **Use a Pre-Assessment**

4. **Check for Understanding**

5. **Assess at the End of Learning**

2025 Creative Leadership Press. This page may be reproduced for classroom use only. All other rights reserved.

DATA-DRIVEN DECISION-MAKING

BIG IDEAS
DATA LITERACY
DATA MINDSET
CAUSE DATA
EFFECT DATA

THIS CHAPTER'S PIECE HELPS US SEE THE FULL PICTURE. DATA-DRIVEN DECISIONS GIVE US insight into what is working, where the gaps are, and how to adjust with intention. In this chapter, we focus on how Collaborative Learning Teams (CLTs) can effectively use data to inform instruction. We'll also introduce a practical framework that teams can use to guide their data discussions and support thoughtful, informed decision-making.

A Data Story

After switching careers and joining my first school, I had data. Data from district benchmark assessments. Data from curriculum-embedded assessments. Data from grades. Data from the state test. Unfortunately, all that data left me feeling like I had made the wrong choice to become a teacher and that I was failing. The reports were shared with me, the results were discussed many times over, and I was exhorted to "do better." I would have done better if I knew how.

Fortunately, I joined a different team the next year. We met regularly, analyzed the standards to build a common understanding of the target of our instruction, shared strategies, reflected on our impact, and adjusted plans. The difference was dramatic. Approximately 30% of my students passed the math state test in my first year, and only one student failed in my second year.

With the volume of data available to educators, it seems we could easily make informed decisions to benefit our students. Unfortunately, it's not always as easy as it seems, and the data often leaves us feeling like we are failing. We share reports and discuss results, but we still hear that we need to do better. Well, if we knew how to do better, we would.

When educators work in Collaborative Learning Teams (CLTs), they learn how to use data to drive instruction. CLTs meet regularly, analyze the learning standards, build a common understanding of learning intentions and success criteria, share strategies, reflect on impact, and adjust plans. Throughout this entire process, the team uses data to make important decisions, which results in data-driven decision-making.

The end of this chapter includes a data analysis discussion guide to help CLT's make the most of their data conversations.

THE WHY

All educators aspire to understand students more deeply to inform instruction. When CLTs discuss and use data to guide their decisions, instruction becomes more intentional and can better meet the needs of every learner. Taking a treasure hunt approach to data helps identify which strategies are working, where students are struggling, and where adjustments are needed.

> "Without [data literacy], data will continue to be a burden to teachers rather than a powerful tool for effective teaching."
>
> —DATA QUALITY CAMPAIGN

Throughout the 30 years of 90/90/90 research, seven common practices emerged across schools that consistently realized gains. One of those practices is constructive data analysis. Reeves observed that "insightful data analysis requires professional collaboration among teachers and agreement about student performance and professional practice" and that "teachers must agree on the fundamental building blocks of student performance—the skills, knowledge, and concepts that together form understanding."[1]

Every student deserves to be taught by a teacher who is part of an effective collaborative team. Data provides a clearer picture of student progress and helps teachers respond in meaningful ways. When we learn to use data effectively, our results can be dramatic.

THE HOW

Data Defined

Schools and classrooms are full of data sources, and narrowing down the type of data is as important as collecting it. Building understanding and driving decision-making with data takes time and intentional effort. While time constraints are real, investing in deep understanding pays off far more than rushing into structures without the necessary foundation.

To really get to the heart of data-driven decision-making, teams must discuss both what the adults are doing (**cause data**) and how the students are responding (**effect data**).

Let's consider the difference:

- **CAUSE DATA** refers to adult behavior and the effectiveness of instructional strategies (i.e., What did the teacher do?).
- **EFFECT DATA** refers to student learning and informs teachers whether their instructional strategies were effective (i.e., What did the student learn as a result of what the teacher did?).

Providing teachers with protocols is a helpful start, but it's just the beginning. True impact comes when educators have the knowledge and confidence to interpret data meaningfully and to apply it thoughtfully. What teachers really need instead of completing data collection forms is a shared framework. They need a different way of thinking about data that helps them make informed, student-centered decisions. By focusing on learning how to use and not simply collect data, CLTs can build a culture where data becomes a tool for growth.

The Data Mindset

A data mindset is a way of thinking and teaching that embraces data as a means to improve teaching and learning. To use data effectively, teachers must be supported with a framework rather than a protocol when thinking about the evidence they have in front of them. Because data is used to make decisions, refine practices, and, ultimately, meet student needs, it should be seen as a tool to inform the learning process and not just a one-time evaluation.

To develop the skills needed to effectively use data, individual team members should continually reflect on the following questions:

- What do all students need?
- What do some students need?
- What do specific students need?

While self-reflection by individuals is key, CLTs can deepen the impact by asking shared questions during data discussions. Effective CLTs use a series of guiding questions such as the following to frame their analysis of data:

- Why are we here?
- What are we looking for?
- Which students know what?
- What will we do about it?

The next section outlines a framework of questions that CLTs can use to maximize their data analysis to guide instruction. The team should work through each of the questions.

THE WHAT

Why are we here? Effective CLTs deliberately remind themselves why they are collaborating. They ask, "Why are we here today with these work samples?" They focus on data from a particular assessment to determine whether students are demonstrating the required knowledge and skills, and they collaboratively plan instruction to move students closer to the previously identified target.

Questions to ask in this step:

- What are we examining today?
- What knowledge and skills should be present?
- Do we have the necessary materials (e.g., work samples, rubrics, success criteria)?

What the conversation might sound like:

> "We are looking at these samples of student work to see if our students can divide fractions by fractions. If not, we are asking what knowledge and skills they do have that we can build on in our upcoming instruction."

PRO TIP

Taking time to focus on what data the team is discussing and how the data impacts the next instructional step requires deliberate focus.

What are we looking for? CLTs begin data-driven decision-making when they analyze and discuss a learning standard(s) to develop learning intentions with clear and measurable success criteria. The criteria serve as the baseline for the assessment, which is designed to precisely measure the concepts and aligned skills outlined in the criteria. The CLT then creates and administers the assessment.

In this part of the data conversation, the CLT uses the predetermined criteria to frame the conversation as they examine evidence of student understanding in the work samples.

Questions to ask in this step:

- What are we assessing?
- What prerequisite knowledge and skills should students be able to apply?
- What knowledge and skills are demanded by the standard?
- What conceptual or procedural understanding is required?

What the conversation might sound like:

> "We are assessing our students' ability to interpret and compute quotients of fractions in regular and word problems. This includes dividing fractions by fractions by using visual models and equations to represent the problem. Students are expected to understand that a fraction represents the division of the numerator by the denominator. Students should use conceptual and procedural understanding to solve the problem. We measured this by asking students to solve the problem, How many 1/8 cup servings can be made from ¾ cup of chocolate?"

Which students know what? What do they need to learn next? In this step, CLTs focus on the stage after the instruction has been planned and students have been assessed. CLT members review the target of the assessment data they have in front of them to answer the question, "Which students need what?"

PRO TIP

Taking time to establish clear criteria provides for better assessment and less ambiguity when evaluating student work.

Teams are often encouraged to score student work before having a discussion; however, effective teams take time to discuss how they will examine and analyze student work samples together rather than just assigning scores before the discussion.

Let's highlight the differences between scoring and analyzing:

SCORING	ANALYZING
• Determines a student's level of performance against a set of clear, explicit criteria. • Does not effectively support collaboration or data-driven instruction when completed individually.	• Views the work sample as evidence of the student's current knowledge and skill. • Allows educators to identify students' strengths and areas for growth.

To quickly identify next steps, CLTs should take a strengths-based approach when examining student work samples. By focusing on what students have already demonstrated, teachers can group learners according to their acquired knowledge and skills. This approach makes it easier to pinpoint remaining learning needs and to define targeted next steps for instruction.

Questions to ask in this step:

- What does the work tell us that students know and can do?
- What does the work tell us about student errors and/or misconceptions?
- What are the patterns in errors and misconceptions?
- Which students have similar needs?

What the conversation might sound like:

> "The first group of students have the basic concept of fractions as part of a whole. We know this because they created separate visual models of 1/8 and 3/4. They need to understand that they are dividing the 3/4 into 1/8 portions or trying to determine how many 1/8 cups there are in 3/4 cups." The CLT would then repeat this analysis for groups to determine what students know and can do.

What will we do about it? Successful CLTs approach this step with a cause-and-effect mindset. Team members ask each other which strategies they can implement (*cause*) to create the desired change in student performance (*effect*). The conversation in this step should focus on how teachers will use the evidence in student work to address opportunities for growth. It is imperative that teachers work together to select the most effective instructional practices that will cause the desired effects.

Questions to ask in this step:

- What is the best instructional strategy to address the errors and/or misconceptions identified by the data?
- What specific instruction will we provide and to which students?

> **PRO TIP**
> Discussing what students currently know and can do offers the clearest path to answering the question, What do students need to learn next?

This step is also an opportunity for teams to distinguish between a strategy and an activity as they respond to students' needs. An instructional strategy is the planned approach to teaching while the activity is the process that facilitates learning.

Effective discussions of strategy include the following:

- Thought processes students need to be engaged in for learning to happen
- Activities students will participate in

What the conversation might sound like:

> "We need this group of students to understand that the goal is to divide 3/4 cup into 1/8 cup servings. To support this, we will pull students into a small group and use fraction tiles to create a physical model to ensure that the fractions are proportional. Students will place 1/8 tiles on top of the three 1/4 tiles to visualize how many 1/8 portions can be made from 3/4 cups. Next, students will draw a corresponding model by using graph paper to represent the fraction tiles. Teachers will then connect the physical representation to the Keep–Change–Flip method, reinforcing the idea that dividing fractions involves determining how many times the second fraction fits into the first. Finally, teachers will model using the reciprocal to demonstrate how dividing fractions is the same as multiplying by a reciprocal."

> **PRO TIP**
> Discussing what students currently know and can do offers the clearest path to answering the question, What do students need to learn next?

ACTION STEPS

Effective collaboration is built through shared purpose, trust, and intentional time together. When engaging in fearless instruction, educators support each other in doing what matters most—helping every student grow.

To make the most of data-driven decision-making, CLTs should do the following:

- ❏ Create an environment where it's safe to take risks, ask questions, and be honest.
- ❏ Develop a shared understanding of standards and what those standards truly ask of students.

DATA-DRIVEN DECISION-MAKING

- ❏ Plan for and follow a cycle for assessment and reflection that drives instruction.
- ❏ Stay open to feedback and support, trusting that collaboration is a skill that grows over time.
- ❏ Learn from challenges and feedback.
- ❏ Celebrate successes.

SECTION I REVIEW

Throughout this section, we explored the power of instructional leadership to lay the foundation for highly effective CLTs that focus on informative assessments and data to positively impact student achievement.

- ▸ In Chapter 1, we examined how instructional leaders can nurture the learning environment and enhance the work of teachers to help them grow professionally and ensure they have the necessary resources.
- ▸ In Chapter 2, we learned about the foundational pieces of highly effective CLTs and the power of teacher collective efficacy. We learned that as teams engage in the CLT process, they use data to focus on standards, assessment, instruction, and differentiation.
- ▸ In Chapter 3, we explored the importance of embedded formative assessment and the planning required to make ongoing checks for understanding a regular part of the learning routine. We reviewed ways to gather multiple sources of data throughout a lesson.
- ▸ In Chapter 4, we continued to refine the practices needed to make data-driven decisions by building off the data collected through embedded formative assessment. In this chapter, we also explored a framework to help build a data mindset and the ability to use data to react to and differentiate for student learning.

REFLECTION QUESTIONS

For leaders:

- ❏ How will I support teacher growth?
- ❏ How can I empower fearless instruction?
- ❏ Do I need to restructure the master schedule?

For all:

- ❏ Is the team focused *equally* on Tier 1 instruction *and* enrichment activity planning? Or is the focus biased toward one or the other?
- ❏ How does the team build opportunities for students to reflect on their learning and assess their progress throughout the lesson?
- ❏ What type of data does the team regularly collect, and how does this impact instructional practices?
- ❏ How do we as individuals or a team assess our learning as educators, and how can we build those ideas into our classrooms?

Data Analysis
DISCUSSION GUIDE

Why are we here?
- What are we examining?
- What knowledge and skills should be present?
- Do we have all necessary materials (e.g., student work samples, scoring guides)?

What are we looking for?
- What knowledge and skills are demanded by the standard?
- What prerequisite knowledge and skills should students be able to apply?
- What conceptual or procedural understanding is required?

Which students know what? What do they need to learn next?
- What does the work tell us that students know and can do?
- What does the work tell us about student errors and/or misconceptions?
- What are the patterns in errors and/or misconceptions?
- Which students have similar needs?

What will we do about it?
- What is the best instructional strategy to address the errors and/or misconceptions identified by the data?
- What specific instruction will we provide and to which students?

— SECTION II —
CONNECTING THE PIECES

Putting the 90/90/90 Research to Work

THE PATH TO RIGOROUS GRADING

BIG IDEAS
HIGH EXPECTATIONS
COGNITIVE ENGAGEMENT
STUDENT MOTIVATION
STUDENT SELF-ASSESSMENT

THIS PIECE ADDS DEPTH TO INSTRUCTIONAL PLANNING AND GRADING PRACTICES, bringing dimension to what might otherwise feel flat. In this chapter, we focus on the path educators take to understand the role of learning and rigor when establishing clear instructional expectations, specifically addressing the question, **How can we ensure we are teaching the standards at their intended level of rigor?** We then examine how those expectations connect to rigorous grading practices to ensure that student grades truly reflect the level of mastery toward standards and, most importantly, how teachers engage students in learning rather than "point earning."

> Educators often hear the need to increase rigor in the classroom. But what does it really mean to provide rigorous instruction? A common description of rigorous lesson material is "intellectually challenging," meaning the degree of difficulty of a lesson or assignment. But when a principal asks a teacher to increase the rigor of instruction, are they really asking the teacher to make it more difficult for students? Or are they asking if the students are ready for more complex tasks?

Just five little letters in the word *rigor*, but so much angst! The concept of rigor can be abstract and complex. The word is often used when discussing instructional practices, but it is rarely defined in an actionable way. It's no surprise that *rigor* appears on many lists of words teachers would like to omit from our vocabulary. Defining rigor through examples contextualizes *what* it is and demonstrates that rigor is not *more,* but *different.*

How Cognitive Rigor Occurs Over Time

Most educational systems use learning standards that build from simple to complex and from concrete to abstract over time. Foundational skills are combined over time to perform more complex functions.

- For example, skip counting in first and second grades introduces the concept of repeated addition, an essential skill for multiplication.
- Then in third and fourth grades, students use those essential skills to perform simple multiplication and division.

Learners may find these skills difficult at first, yet they are not complex. As students show mastery of the simple skills, they gain confidence, helping them to persevere as they learn multidigit multiplication and long division. These surface processes help students understand what it means to multiply or divide before they begin tackling deeper tasks such as the division or multiplication of fractions and decimals.

Those same skills that were taught in elementary school are then transferred for use in later math courses to solve complex problems.

- For example, students model a linear relationship with independent and dependent variables, such as the cost of calculating a taxi ride that includes a base fare and mileage charge.

In this last example, students are not blindly applying formulas. Instead, they are asking themselves if their answer makes sense. They use multiple approaches or break the problem into multiple steps. Students who have the best understanding are those who can think both strategically and flexibly about the complex problem they are trying to solve.

This is cognitive rigor.

The end of this chapter includes a sample holistic rubric as a model for rigorous grading. This exemplar shows rigor embedded in the "4" while providing clear criteria for feedback and improvement. The rubric also includes a planning guide to help your team reflect and plan a path to rigorous grading.

THE WHY

Educators want rich learning experiences for their students, so they set goals for achievement and work diligently to achieve them. When achievement goals are unmet or learning opportunities have limited depth, the reason is usually a lack of cognitive rigor. Instructional rigor emphasizes learning experiences that promote deep thinking and understanding rather than simply increasing the difficulty or amount of work. The role of rigor in teaching and learning is directly connected to understanding what the content standards are asking students to know and be able to do and to what level.

Whether your school district uses state standards or local performance objectives, there is likely a document or guide that defines the expectation for what is taught in each grade level and content area. One of the greatest sources of frustration that leaders hear from teachers is that there are too many standards.

- For example, in most US states there are about 200 English Language Arts standards in kindergarten through grade 12. And this is just one content area!

With a 180-day instructional calendar, it's not realistic to think that all standards can be effectively taught in a year. Therefore, rigorous grading starts with deeply understanding the learning process beginning with the standard to be taught and identifying what it will look and sound like when students demonstrate proficiency.

THE HOW

To foster rigorous learning, teachers begin planning with learning at the forefront. This directly connects to the work of CLTs when establishing learning intentions and determining evidence of student understanding.

Identify the Phase of Learning
Start the process by considering where students are in their learning and deciding on the correct type of strategy to use when teaching. Begin with identifying the correct learning phase.

Hattie's Stages of Learning

John Hattie and Gregory Donoghue present educators with a familiar model of cognitive rigor that captures how students move through three phases of learning: surface, deep, and transfer.[1]

1. **Surface learning** involves acquiring foundational knowledge and understanding the basic concepts, facts, and vocabulary. Surface learning provides the necessary groundwork for deeper understanding.
2. **Deep learning** involves making connections between ideas, developing conceptual understanding, and applying knowledge to new situations within a similar context.
3. **Transfer learning**, the ultimate goal, involves learners applying their knowledge and skills to novel situations and contexts beyond the initial learning environment. It requires a deep understanding and the ability to think metacognitively, reflecting on one's learning and understanding.

> **PRO TIP**
> In the classroom, this can look like direct instruction with notetaking at the beginning of a unit that moves into concept mapping and, finally, reciprocal teaching as students gain confidence with the topic. The unit could end with student presentations using real-life applications of the concepts learned.

Hattie and Donoghue's model demonstrates how instructional rigor moves from simple to complex.

Stages of Learning Simplified

The progression from surface to deep to transfer learning directly affects cognitive engagement. Let's look at an easier way to remember these familiar stages:

1. **Surface learning:** Students learn the **skill**.
2. **Deep learning:** Students gain confidence in their learning, which Hattie and Donoghue call the **will.**
3. **Transfer learning:** Students apply their learning in new situations and experience the **thrill** of learning, often known as the "a-ha moment."

Hattie's research provides the framework to categorize student stages of learning in the context of rigor. However, discussing rigor can be more complex than just the three stages of learning. Given the inherent ambiguity in many learning standards, educators need a more descriptive tool when discussing rigor, evaluating activities, and setting learning expectations. The Hess Cognitive Rigor Matrix provides the level of detail teams may need to clearly evaluate and discuss rigor in the context of learning.

FEARLESS INSTRUCTION

Evaluate Standards, Assignments, and Assessments for Rigor

Karin Hess's Cognitive Rigor Matrix is a widely used instructional planning tool for assessing the rigor of standards.[2] It also helps teachers evaluate the rigor of assignments and assessments while providing ideas for scaffolding the learning or extending thinking and content knowledge.

Hess's Cognitive Rigor Matrix

This matrix integrates Bloom's Revised Taxonomy and Webb's Depth of Knowledge (DOK) to create a framework that emphasizes the intersection of cognitive demand and content complexity ensuring that tasks not only cover what students should know, but also how they think and apply that knowledge.

> Let's do a quick review:
> - Bloom's Taxonomy provides a hierarchy of cognitive processes involved in learning, ranging from remembering factual information to creating new knowledge. This hierarchy helps teachers consider the type of **thinking** students are engaged in during a task.[3]
> - Webb's Depth of Knowledge (DOK) focuses on the complexity of the content and the level of understanding required to successfully complete a task. DOK levels range from recall and reproduction to extended thinking. As DOK levels increase, the **content knowledge** increases.[4]

Because rigor is one of the most misunderstood words in education, let's combine these ideas to create a definition that is simpler and easier to understand and remember.

Thinking + Content Knowledge = Rigor

In addition to using the matrix for planning, Hess suggests that teachers set the following expectations for instruction:

- Evaluate the level of thinking and content understanding required to be successful with the learning objective.
- Design learning experiences and assessments that move beyond simple recall and encourage deeper levels of analysis, evaluation, and creation with complex content.

THE PATH TO RIGOROUS GRADING

- Understand the relationship between thinking processes and content knowledge and how different levels of cognitive demand interact with varying depths of knowledge.

> The Cognitive Rigor Matrix is a tool that teachers can use to evaluate their standards, tasks, or assessments. It can be used by CLTs to understand the rigor or their standards and enhance their collaborative discussion. As CLT's evaluate their standards using the matrix it helps them define proficiency and plan for differentiation. For purposes of this chapter, proficiency becomes the "3" in a 4-point grading scale.

Hess's work reminds us that much of the art of teaching is in the design of learning. Investing time to analyze learning standards in terms of cognitive demand and content knowledge allows teachers to focus their instruction. This is best achieved when teacher teams collaboratively build a set of Power Standards™ to truly focus their curriculum and develop instruction at the intended level of rigor for their grade level or subject matter progression. (See the introduction for more about Power Standards.)

Applying our learning from Hess's body of work, we can look at both the cognitive processes and the complexity of the knowledge required in each grade.

Let's look at an example of the progression of a third grade reading standard:

GRADE 3	GRADE 4	GRADE 5
Ask and answer questions to demonstrate understanding of a text, referring explicitly to the text as the basis for the answers.	Refer to details and examples in a text when explaining what the text says explicitly and when drawing inferences from the text.	Quote accurately from a text when explaining what the text says explicitly and when drawing inferences from the text.

- As third grade teachers plan instruction, they know they will be guiding students through asking and answering questions about explicit details in the text.
- Fourth grade teachers will build on that foundation by drawing out details that are not expressly stated in the text.
- Fifth grade teachers will add a layer of critical thinking by asking students to quote both explicit and inferred examples.

If teachers in earlier or later grades plan and teach a standard with too much or too little rigor, they create inconsistencies that the next teacher must address. This is not to say that we don't differentiate learning for students, but the goal is for students to master that year's standard as the foundation for the next. A practical way to measure progress toward mastery is by developing and communicating success criteria. (See Chapter 6 for more about success criteria.)

> Success criteria provide the framework for the level of rigor in the classroom by clearly defining proficiency. To define the rigor needed for both teaching and learning, a CLT asks, "What does success with this standard look like and sound like?" Success criteria must be carefully predetermined based on learning intentions or standards and clearly communicated to students.

Communicate the Expectations

Rigorous learning is fostered by communicating success criteria and giving students opportunities to present evidence of their learning. As students begin to meet the success criteria, teachers can introduce how to take learning to the next level.

As teachers shift from planning learning to delivering instruction, the success criteria move to the forefront. Sharing with students in advance what it will take to show proficiency with the required skills and concepts provides a foundation on which students can anchor their learning progress. If students know what proficiency looks like, working toward that clear expectation feels much more doable.

Teachers and students alike get feedback from success criteria. If students are not making progress toward the expectation, the feedback tells the teacher that the skill or concept needs to be taught in a different way. If students are struggling with just one part of the success criteria, they can be specific in their request for assistance.

A clear picture of proficiency

- provides feedback to both students and teachers,
- brings into focus what students need to know and do,
- creates space to ensure lessons and activities are aligned with those specific needs, and
- saves teachers time and energy.

> For example, if a student needs to show proficiency by setting up and conducting an investigation, the teacher should provide multiple opportunities to set up and conduct investigations. There is no need for long lectures about investigation procedures or vocabulary drills. What students do need are plenty of opportunities to design, do, and report on investigations, and they need FAST Feedback. (See Chapter 8 for more on feedback.)

Rigorous learning in an investigation can happen in two ways:

- Students start with simple investigations to understand the skill and then move to more complex investigations, which induce a thrill.
- Using the gradual release model, teachers provide more support at the beginning of the learning process and gradually shift responsibility to students as they develop independence.

As students participate in and have some control over their learning, they gain motivation. This is not to say that every student magically brings their A-game to the classroom. However, many students do reengage when instruction is directly connected to clearly communicated expectations.

THE WHAT

It's Not About the Points

How to plan for and implement rigorous teaching leads to the *what* for implementing rigorous grading. Rigorous grading ensures that students have multiple opportunities to use the success criteria to reflect on their work and to make adjustments to improve their skills. (For a full text on grading, see *Fearless Grading* by Douglas Reeves.)

Feedback happens throughout rigorous instruction, with both the teacher and the learner referring often to the success criteria. Grading happens less often, usually at the end of an instructional period such as a unit or term.

When discussing grading, it is common to hear that points earned determine the grade received. When asked how points measure a student's learning, most teachers answer that points represent a percentage of "right" answers or products (i.e., getting seven of ten questions correct on a quiz). Sometimes factored in are points that are deducted for late work or points that are added for doing extra credit.

When teachers and CLTs shift to using success criteria to grade, they create the condition for students to shift their perspective from point-gathering to self-assessing. A rubric or checklist is a common strategy to present success criteria to students who can then self-assess based on FAST Feedback throughout the learning process. (See Chapter 8 for more about feedback.)

When using self-assessment in grading, the teacher agrees or disagrees with the student's evaluation and provides feedback as needed. This process invites students to think about what they need to do to show their understanding of the skills and concepts being taught. Grades are then based on progress toward the standard, rather than points accumulated. (See Chapter 6 for more on rubrics and self-assessment.)

FEARLESS INSTRUCTION

> **"If your culture is comfortable with letter grades, then keep letter grades. Just make them accurate."**
>
> —DOUGLAS REEVES

Rigorous grading does not need to be overly complicated. In *Fearless Grading*, Reeves proposes that the key discussion points of grading reform are fairness and accuracy rather than the letters or numbers assigned to work.[5] Reeves suggests that the heart of rigorous grading is providing your community with language that is clearly defined.

Sample language for rigorous grading:

	RIGOROUS GRADING	
4 OR A	EXEMPLARY	The student demonstrates thinking and content knowledge that is greater in complexity than meeting the grade level standard or success criteria.
3 OR B	PROFICIENT	The student demonstrates understanding of the content and achieves expected outcomes for the grade level standard or success criteria.
2 OR C	PROGRESSING	The student demonstrates partial understanding of the content and is showing growth toward the grade level standard or success criteria.
1 OR D	APPROACHING	The student demonstrates minimal understanding of the content and needs direct support to progress toward meeting the grade level standard or success criteria.
0 OR F	INSUFFICIENT EVIDENCE	The student is not yet demonstrating evidence of understanding related to the grade level standard or success criteria.

Applying Rigorous Grading to Real Life

Let's consider grading in the context of a holistic rubric. A holistic rubric evaluates student work as a whole, resulting in an overall score rather than an average. Developing a holistic rubric begins first with the CLT defining what proficiency of the standard is, using the Hess Matrix to define the "3." Defining proficiency in this way helps the team ensure that rigor is built of the conversation. The team then develops the rest of the rubric from the 3.

> **Steps to developing a holistic rubric for rigorous grading:**
>
> 1. Start with what it looks like if students meet the objective. The labels may vary, but we'll define this as "Proficient," often represented as a B or a 3.
> 2. Define what it looks like when students apply their knowledge in a new way to show that they deeply understood the skills and concepts of the standard. This might be called "Exceeds the Standard" or "Exemplary" and is typically the grade that is the equivalent of an A or a 4. CLTs often get stuck establishing the difference between Proficient and Exemplary.
> 3. Determine what it looks like if students are close but not quite proficient, which we'll call "Progressing," represented as a C or a 2.
> 4. Identify what it looks like when students have shown some skill or concept knowledge, but improvements are inconsistent or limited. We define this as "Approaching," represented as a D or a 1.
> 5. The lowest grade category reflects no evidence of mastery, usually because the work is incomplete or not completed, and is often represented as an F or a 0. We label this "Insufficient Evidence" because the teacher does not have enough to grade.

Holistic Rubric for Feedback and Grading

Let's look at a holistic rubric used for feedback and grading through a standard that applies to most grades and content areas: writing an argumentative essay. By the time students reach sixth grade, they have been writing opinion essays for a few years. The shift to argumentative writing requires students to state a claim and then support that claim with reasoning and evidence.

As students progress through the assignment, the teacher uses the success criteria to provide feedback for improvement, shifting the focus from points earned to content learned.

- A student who scores **Proficient** does so by clearly making connections between the claim and the reasoning and evidence.
- Students who receive a score of **Exemplary** meet the criteria for Proficient, but their claims are insightful or nuanced, they include a counterclaim and refute it, their language is precise, and they ensured their paper was neatly presented.

- A student who is **Progressing** or **Approaching** is missing some or many of these components, as explicitly defined in the success criteria, and these grades are fairly easy to identify and justify.

A final thought. There has been a lot of discussion in recent years about grading scales and grading policies, but teachers and CLTs do not need to wait for districts to take on a large-scale initiative. The collective power of CLTs to determine proficiency, discuss rigor, collaboratively develop criteria and rubrics, and engage in collaborative scoring are strategies that can be implemented immediately.

ACTION STEPS

- ❏ Plan for rigorous teaching by deeply understanding the standard and identifying what it will look and sound like when students meet the standard.
- ❏ Foster rigorous learning by communicating the success criteria and then giving students opportunities to present evidence of their learning. As students begin to meet the success criteria, teachers can introduce how to take the learning to the next level.
- ❏ Implement rigorous grading by ensuring that students have multiple opportunities to use the success criteria to reflect on their work and make adjustments to improve their skills.

THE PATH TO RIGOROUS GRADING

Explore the steps of planning and implementing rigorous instruction and grading with your CLT. To create the action plan, consider the learning that will happen and the best strategies for the learning phase. When discussing the feedback plan, consider how to best communicate expectations and provide frequent feedback, keeping in mind that feedback ends with grading.

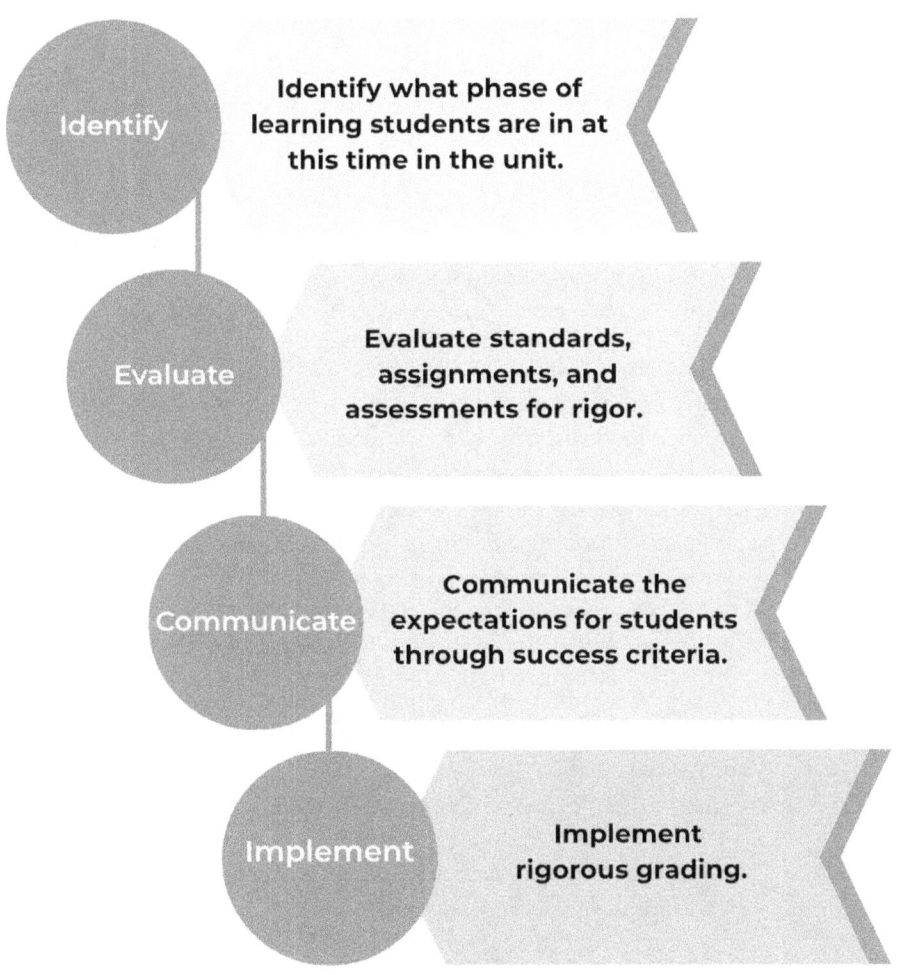

Identify — Identify what phase of learning students are in at this time in the unit.

Evaluate — Evaluate standards, assignments, and assessments for rigor.

Communicate — Communicate the expectations for students through success criteria.

Implement — Implement rigorous grading.

6TH GRADE ARGUMENTATIVE ESSAY HOLISTIC RUBRIC

SCORE	SUCCESS CRITERIA
4—EXEMPLARY	❏ The student meets all Proficient criteria and goes beyond. ❏ Claim is clear, insightful or nuanced, showing depth of thought. ❏ Evidence and reasoning are directly connected to claim. ❏ Counterclaim is included and refuted, demonstrating awareness of multiple perspectives. ❏ Language is precise and purposeful, enhancing the argument. ❏ Writing includes a clear voice and a command of conventions.

3—PROFICIENT	❏ Clear and focused claim supported by at least 3 pieces of evidence with relevant reasoning.
	❏ Evidence is cited correctly and clearly supports the claim.
	❏ Types of evidence may include facts, examples, quotes, data, etc.
	❏ Organization is logical and easy to follow. Includes all of the following:
	   • Introduction that includes the claim
	   • Multiple (at least 3) supporting paragraphs that expand on each reason
	   • Transitions between paragraphs
	   • Conclusion that restates the claim and summarizes key points
	   • Language is appropriate and effective
	❏ Conventions are mostly correct; errors do not interfere with meaning.

2—PROGRESSING	❏ Contains a claim, but it is not clear.
	❏ Contains less than 3 pieces of evidence and reasoning is loosely connected.
	❏ Evidence is inconsistently cited correctly. Organization is inconsistent or confusing. Missing one or more of the following:
	   • Introduction that includes the claim
	   • At least 3 supporting paragraphs that expand on each reason
	   • Transitions between paragraphs
	   • Conclusion that restates the claim and summarizes key points
	❏ Errors in conventions interfere with meaning at least 25% of the time.

1—APPROACHING	❏ Writing lacks a clear claim or argument; it may be off-topic or undeveloped.
	❏ Contains less than 2 pieces of evidence that are off topic or unrelated; support is unclear or missing.
	❏ Organization is inconsistent or confusing. Missing two or more of the following:
	   • Introduction that includes the claim
	   • At least 3 supporting paragraphs that expand on each reason
	   • Transitions between paragraphs
	   • Conclusion that restates the claim and summarizes key points
	❏ Errors in conventions interfere with meaning at least 50% of the time.

2025 Creative Leadership Press. This page may be reproduced for classroom use only. All other rights reserved.

BIG IDEAS
TEACHER CLARITY
RUBRICS
EXEMPLAR
CALIBRATION

RUBRICS AND COLLABORATIVE SCORING
Clear Criteria for Quality Student Work

THIS PIECE CONNECTS THE EDGES, BRINGING STRUCTURE AND CLARITY TO YOUR instruction. In this chapter, we will learn how to create and communicate clear, specific expectations. We will explore how teacher clarity provides a framework for the important teaching tasks of analyzing standards, creating learning intentions and success criteria, and developing rubrics for assessment and feedback. Lastly, we will examine how these practices support Collaborative Learning Teams (CLTs) in calibrating expectations and engaging in collaborative scoring.

Students need consistency of expectations that are crafted with careful planning, execution, and practice. Whether writing the thesis of an essay, completing a graph for a mathematical task, conducting an experiment of mold in an ecosystem, or painting a self-portrait in art, students need to know the expectations. To meet these expectations and reach proficiency, students need time, practice, and a clear path to get there.

Hattie defines clear and consistent expectations for students as teacher clarity.[1] With an effect size of 0.85, teacher clarity has the potential to have twice the impact of an average year of schooling for students. Clarity tells students where they are going in their learning and how they will know they have achieved the target.[2]

For students, clarity in the classroom starts with

- clear expectations of what they are learning,
- why they are learning it, and
- how they will show they have learned it.

For teachers, creating clarity for students starts with

- understanding the most important parts of the standards,
- identifying the concepts and aligned skills,
- defining what students should master within the standards,
- writing specific learning intentions, and
- creating success criteria to support students and clarify expectations.

The power of teacher clarity is best demonstrated when the CLT comes together to analyze standards and collectively agree on the expectations for learning. The CLT then calibrates their expectations and engages in collaborative scoring. This process allows the CLT to know if there is enough clarity in their criteria and rubric. The last section of this chapter will help CLTs engage in that practice.

The end of this chapter includes a collaborative scoring protocol for your CLTs.

> *This chapter introduces a process for creating teacher clarity in planning, grading, and feedback and assumes that Power Standards™ are already established. (See the introduction for a primer on Power Standards.)*

THE WHY

Good work. We expect it from ourselves, and we want it from our students. It is what students want for themselves too. Unfortunately, the path to good work is not always clear. When students can't connect where they currently are in their learning to where they need to go, they can be left overwhelmed and unable to even start. They are left with questions such as these: How do I meet the requirements that have been set? What, specifically, do I need to do? What does good work even look like?

There can be a vast divide between the expectations set by the teacher and the actionable steps students need to reach them. This gap in understanding causes students to sometimes avoid doing any

RUBRICS AND COLLABORATIVE SCORING

work at all, or more frequently, making guesses about what is required, only to fall short. Teachers must work hard to ensure consistency and quality in their teaching to support student learning.

The next section defines the process teachers and CLTs can use to create clarity through unpacking Power Standards to creating learning intentions and success criteria.

THE HOW

Break Down the Standard

The first step of the process is analyzing and breaking down a standard to identify the concepts and aligned skills that students should master. This step helps your team gain a deeper understanding of what students are expected to learn and do.

POWER STANDARD	
Example: Identify whether the number of objects in one group is greater than, less than, or equal to the number of objects in another group, e.g., by using matching and counting strategies.	
CONCEPTS	**ALIGNED SKILLS**
What content do the students have to understand to demonstrate proficiency on this standard? *Examples:* • *groups of objects* • *greater than* • *less than* • *equal to* • *matching strategies* • *counting strategies*	What do the students have to be able to do to demonstrate proficiency on this standard? *Examples:* • *Identify if two groups of objects are equal.* • *Identify which group is greater and which is less.* • *Use matching to compare.* • *Use counting to compare.*

Create Clarity for Success

The second step in the process is to create clarity for student success. Once the standard is fully understood, it can then be broken down into the teachable components. This step concludes by clarifying expectations through specific learning intentions and success criteria to support students in their learning.

FEARLESS INSTRUCTION

Learning Intentions

The learning intentions combine the concepts and aligned skills to create a statement for learning. As CLTs write learning intentions, the following questions can be used to guide thinking:

- Why do students need to know this?
- What are the teachable components of the standard?
- What are the lesson-sized "chunks" of learning?

When shared with students at the beginning of a lesson, learning intentions provide a powerful frame for learning. When writing learning intentions, begin the statements with "I am learning to" to create student-friendly language.

Success Criteria

After writing the learning intentions, CLTs can clarify expectations further by determining what students need to do to demonstrate proficiency for that component of the standard- success criteria. Success criteria are specific and observable indicators that outline what students must demonstrate as evidence of learning.

> **Consider the following questions when writing and evaluating success criteria:**
>
> - What evidence will students show to demonstrate their understanding?
> - Will the criteria outline a process, product, or conceptual understanding?
> - What vocabulary or accountable talk will the students use when they demonstrate understanding?
> - Are the criteria clear, leaving nothing to chance?
> - Are the criteria measurable?

Because success criteria are intended to be used with students, they are frequently written as "I can" statements. Each success criteria is a step in the learning progression and provides the road map students need for learning.

An effective way to create clarity is to write learning intentions and success criteria at the same time. Use the phrase "I am learning to…" followed by "so that I can …" to combine them, making it easier to write clear, focused statements.

Let's build on our kindergarten example and look at sample combined learning intentions and success criteria. These statements are built from the concepts and aligned skills that were identified in the previous example of an analyzed standard.

POWER STANDARD

Example: Identify whether the number of objects in one group is greater than, less than, or equal to the number of objects in another group, e.g., by using matching and counting strategies.

CONCEPTS	ALIGNED SKILLS
What content do the students have to understand to demonstrate proficiency on this standard?	What do the students have to be able to do to demonstrate proficiency on this standard?
Examples: • groups of objects • greater than • less than • equal to • matching strategies • counting strategies	Examples: • Identify if two groups of objects are equal. • Identify which group is greater and which is less. • Use matching to compare. • Use counting to compare.

LEARNING INTENTIONS AND SUCCESS CRITERIA

Learning intentions create a statement for learning by combining concepts and aligned skills. Success criteria are specific and observable indicators that outline what students must demonstrate as evidence of learning.

In the following examples, the learning intentions start with "I am learning to," and the success criteria start with "I can":

- I am learning to compare two groups of objects to see which has more, less, or an equal number so that …
    - I can count the number of objects in each group.
    - I can line up and match corresponding objects in each group.
    - I can identify which group has more, less, or the same number.
- I am learning to explain how I compared the size of two groups using matching and counting so that …
    - I can explain if a group has more, less, or the same as another group after counting and matching objects.
    - I can explain what I did to compare the groups.

It is also powerful to provide students with examples of exemplary work. When teachers model skills and guide students in evaluating examples by using the level of specificity in the success criteria, students better understand the expected end product.

FEARLESS INSTRUCTION

Benefits of using models:

- Creates opportunities for students to work and practice alongside their teacher.
- Creates opportunities for students to work and practice alongside their peers.
- Builds deeper understanding as individuals.

Build Rubrics with Clarity

Once CLTs have analyzed standards and created clarity, they are ready to begin the third step in the process: building rubrics. Rubrics are tools designed to accurately measure the quality of student work and to ensure fairness, measuring the evidence of learning provided by students against specific success criteria.

The Rubric Panic

Put yourself in the mind and body of your students. You have just been handed a sheet of paper, and here is what you see:

- A 4 X 5 grid with each of the boxes filled with words
- The numbers 0 to 4 or words like *Advanced*, *Proficient*, and *Emerging* in the top row
- A list of categories in the left-hand column
- Words like *thorough*, *adequate*, *significant*, *mostly*

As you scan the page to figure out the requirements for your work, panic starts to set in as you read for something simple that you actually understand how to do. You now want to do the least that is required to get this task over with!

This scenario is a reality for many of our students. Unfortunately, many rubrics are too wordy and overcomplicated for both teachers and students to understand and use.[3] Most rubrics indicate how well students meet specific expectations. However, when aligned to specific success criteria that measures student learning, rubrics help teachers evaluate the quality of student work more effectively.

Rubrics are most powerful when used as a means for feedback to improve student work. Instead of an overly complicated rubric that mystifies students, teachers should provide language that establishes clear expectations for students and that can be applied accurately and fairly across all student work.

Let's examine the differences between these two sample criteria used to evaluate an essay:

EXAMPLE 1	EXAMPLE 2
Provides thorough evidence to support claim.	Provides 3 to 5 pieces of evidence that explicitly link to the claim.

Which example might leave students guessing? Which one are students more likely to understand and be able to do?

- Example 1 is ambiguous and does not clearly define "thorough."
- Example 2 provides more clarity, leaves out vague language, and can be applied accurately and fairly across all pieces of work completed.

Provide Only the Desired Outcome

Let's revisit the rubric with 20 squares on the page. On most rubrics like this, two of the four columns describe work that meets the expectation (or better) of the standard or is acceptable. The other two or three columns include work that does not acceptably meet the standard. If what is included is not acceptable, why are there descriptions on the rubric that have that quality of work as an option? Many of us have encountered students who are looking to only do the minimum. To motivate students to achieve at the desired outcome, try using additional columns to provide feedback to students. (See Chapter 8 for more on feedback.)

> **PRO TIP**
>
> Clear up ambiguous language on rubrics, and then only give students the columns that meet expectations. If the other columns do not define the quality of work you desire, remove them from the rubric presented to students.

Additional benefits for students and teachers:

- When students have rubrics that contain clear language, they produce higher quality work because they understand the expectations.
- Students can use the rubric to self-assess if they have included all necessary components.
- Peers can apply the rubric to provide an additional layer of assessment and feedback.

By the time the work reaches the teacher, it has been through two reviews. This typically results in higher quality work being handed in because missing or incomplete areas have most likely been addressed. This process also saves teachers time because it takes less time to score and give feedback on quality work.

FEARLESS INSTRUCTION

Once clear success criteria are established, the rubric becomes a flexible tool for providing feedback or for student self-assessment. The level of proficiency as defined by the success criteria becomes the basis for feedback and grading.

Flexible Rubrics

Let's explore two examples of flexible rubrics that are created directly from success criteria: three-column rubrics and single-point rubrics. These types of rubrics offer a simplified way to apply success criteria and to facilitate better feedback.

Three-Column Rubric

The three-column rubric is predominantly used for student self-assessment and teacher feedback. It can also be used for peer feedback.

> **PRO TIP**
>
> Have students apply the rubrics to sample tasks and calibrate with their peers and teachers to raise their levels of understanding. This practice helps students create better work products.

- The first column lists the success criteria—what strong work looks like—written in student-friendly language.
- The second column provides space for students to self-reflect and assess whether they met each expectation. Require students to write in full sentences and justify how they rated themselves.
- The third column is reserved for teacher feedback, but only in areas where the teacher's feedback differs from the student's self-assessment. If teachers agree, they put a check mark.

Sample 3-column rubric:

3-COLUMN RUBRIC		
SUCCESS CRITERIA	SELF-ASSESSMENT	TEACHER FEEDBACK
I read the text by myself.		
I wrote 3 different types of questions that can be answered by reading the text.		
I correctly answered questions about the text in complete sentences,		
I cited 3 pieces of evidence from the text in my answer.		

Single-Point Rubric

The single-point rubric, as advocated by Jennifer Gonzalez,[4] is another way to use success criteria to provide feedback and to engage students in the process.

- The middle column lists the success criteria.
- The left column provides feedback for growth or areas that need refinement.
- The right column provides feedback for students who are working above proficiency.

Sample single-point rubric:

SINGLE-POINT RUBRIC		
GROWTH OPPORTUNITIES Areas that Need Refinement	**SUCCESS CRITERIA** Requirements for Success	**ADVANCED** Evidence Beyond Success Criteria
	I read the text by myself.	
	I wrote 3 different types of questions that can be answered by reading the text.	
	I correctly answered questions about the text in complete sentences.	
	I cited 3 pieces of evidence from the text in my answer.	

Students need clear criteria to produce high-quality work, and teachers need clear criteria to provide feedback for assessment and growth. Too frequently we overcomplicate what should be simple. Simplifying rubrics and using uncomplicated, understandable criteria boosts students' capacity to complete "good" work and can greatly reduce the time teachers spend grading.

THE WHAT

Take a moment to step out of your classroom and into your favorite restaurant. What makes your favorite meal so satisfying? How do chefs ensure that we have the same delicious experience each time that plate is placed in front of us? Consistency. Great restaurants rely on precise recipes, step-by-step guides that ensure every dish meets expectations, no matter who prepares it. When a recipe is understood and followed precisely, any chef who desires to cook that dish can do so to the expectation because of the specificity contained in the ingredient list and instructions. The result is good food every time!

Now, step back into the classroom. Just like line cooks develop skills through observation, practice, and feedback, students need the same to master academic tasks, whether it's writing a thesis, solving a math problem, or creating art. Quality work requires time, training, and clear guidance.

As established throughout this book, clear learning criteria are essential for effective teaching and assessment. Rubrics that clearly define expectations not only guide students but also support teachers in collaborative scoring, the focus of this section. When CLTs align their expectations and score student work together, they promote fairness, accuracy, and consistency in grading. With clear criteria in place, student achievement is rooted in the standards and expectations, not the physical classroom or which teacher grades the work.

Quality Control Through Collaboration and Calibration

Let's revisit our favorite restaurants. Just as successful restaurants expand to new locations and train their staff to maintain the same high-quality and consistency, schools should calibrate instruction across classrooms to ensure all students receive the same high-quality learning experience. Finding a restaurant brand where we have dined before sets up that same expectation for our favorite meals. Creating clear rubrics creates consistent opportunities for meaningful feedback, and collaborative scoring aligns expectations across the building.

Because collaborative scoring is an effective process for calibrating expectations and checking the reliability of rubrics, CLTs can feel confident in their rubrics. The collaborative scoring process can be used with any performance task or assessment that requires the use of a scoring guide, such as the following:

- Essays
- Math problem-solving

- Lab reports
- Demonstrations

Note that when engaging in collaborative scoring, 80% of teachers in the CLT should agree on the score.[5] If the CLT does not agree, they should revisit the criteria in the rubric. In most instances, four work samples will be sufficient to complete the collaborative scoring steps within the allotted time for professional learning. If participants are new to the collaborative scoring process or hesitant to have their students' work reviewed, the facilitator can use anonymous samples that are prepared in advance.

The Collaborative Scoring Steps guide that follows provides five steps CLTs can use to engage with the powerful tool of collaborative scoring.

ACTION STEPS

- ❏ Collaborate regularly with colleagues to identify essential concepts and aligned skills students need to learn.
- ❏ Agree on what proficiency looks like for each key concept or skill.
- ❏ Calibrate expectations with your team to ensure consistency in instruction and feedback.
- ❏ Participate in collaborative scoring of student work to align grading and deepen shared understanding of quality.
- ❏ Practice writing clear learning intentions and success criteria and seek feedback to improve clarity.
- ❏ Work with a coach or peer to refine how you communicate expectations to students.
- ❏ Use collaborative time to reflect on how your clarity impacts student work and engagement.

Collaborative Scoring Steps

01 SCORE INDIVIDUALLY
Each participant receives the same anonymous student work and scoring guide (rubric or checklist) to score independently without discussion.

02 REVIEW RESULTS
The facilitator collects scores and summarizes the distribution (e.g., 20% gave it a 4; 30% gave it a 3).

03 DISCUSS DIFFERENCES
Participants explain their scores and note disagreements, which are often tied to unclear rubric language.

04 CLARIFY AND ADJUST
The group refines the scoring guide to increase clarity and consistency.

05 RESCORE FOR AGREEMENT
Participants use the revised guide to rescore the work, repeating the process until 80% of the group agrees on a score.

BIG IDEAS

BIG IDEAS
EXPLANATORY
INFORMATIVE
MOTIVATION
ALIGNMENT
VERTICAL ARTICULATION

NONFICTION WRITING
Transforming Writing from Fear to Fire

THIS PIECE FILLS IN AN EXCITING DETAIL TO THE PICTURE—NONFICTION WRITING HELPS students make sense of their learning and show what they know in every content area. This chapter explores the power of nonfiction writing and the alignment and collaboration strategies that strengthen its impact across grade levels and content areas. Elevating student writing through nonfiction is not just about teaching a set of skills, it's about creating a learning environment where teachers feel confident as writing instructors and students feel empowered to express themselves. By embracing high expectations, aligning instructional strategies, and implementing motivating classroom practices, we can ignite a passion for writing that extends far beyond the classroom.

Across all the 90/90/90 data, schools who engaged in nonfiction writing across the curriculum saw higher gains in student achievement. Nonfiction writing is a high-leverage strategy that incorporates rigorous expectations, clear success criteria, and quality rubrics.

Nonfiction writing in the classroom incorporates a wide range of genres and purposes. Rooted in real-world topics, facts, and ideas, it provides students with opportunities to think critically, communicate clearly, and reflect on their learning across the curriculum. In the classroom, nonfiction writing includes the following types of writing:

- **Informational Writing:** This genre teaches students to use evidence from sources to explain a topic clearly and accurately. Students may write reports, articles, or explanatory essays, often connected to learning in science, social studies, or other subjects.
- **Opinion and Argument Writing:** This genre allows students to use evidence to make a claim to persuade their audience. This type of writing helps students develop reasoning skills and learn how to persuasively articulate their voice and perspective.
- **Personal Narrative:** Allowing students to share their own experiences helps them connect their lives to the broader world and feel seen and valued. Providing opportunities to share their writing with peers builds a sense of community and fosters empathy in the classroom.
- **Biographical Writing:** This form of informational writing invites students to research someone's life, gaining insight into their experiences and impact. It strengthens research skills and helps students craft engaging, evidence-based narratives.
- **Procedural Writing:** Writing step-by-step instructions sharpens students' attention to detail, sequencing, and audience needs. It integrates seamlessly with science, STEAM, and hands-on learning.
- **Reflective Writing:** One of the most effective ways to build metacognition—thinking about one's own thinking—is through reflective writing. When students pause to reflect, they make deeper meaning of their experiences, reinforcing and internalizing what they have learned.

We've all been in that staff meeting when the latest high-stakes state assessment results are revealed. A clear pattern emerges: Students in classrooms where high expectations are the norm consistently achieve at the highest levels. Many of us feel disappointed, overwhelmed, or even embarrassed by our students' performance, but the purpose of sharing results is not to compare but to show what is possible when students are truly believed in and consistently challenged to do their best work.

One powerful example comes from a teacher who consistently saw remarkable results year after year. When she transitioned from teaching sixth grade to third grade, her students still outperformed expectations across the board. Her secret? She humbly says, "I just expect a lot from my students." But high expectations alone don't tell us the whole story. Yes, she held every student to a high standard, but she also made nonfiction writing a regular part of instruction. The results spoke for themselves, not just in writing, but in reading, math, and science as well. Her approach proved that when high expectations are paired with a focus on writing, student success follows, no matter the grade level.

The end of this chapter includes a guide for CLTs to use when planning for nonfiction writing.

THE WHY

Research shows that when students regularly engage with nonfiction writing, their performance improves not only in writing but also across subjects like reading, math, and science.[1] It is no surprise, then, that teachers with outstanding student achievement year after year not only incorporate nonfiction writing daily but have unwavering high expectations for student writing.

So why don't we see this same emphasis on nonfiction writing in every classroom across the country? From coast to coast, teachers share that teaching writing is scary and intimidating. They often question their own writing skills and are unsure how to instruct students to get the best results.

Additionally, as students travel through the grade levels, they begin to view writing as a torturous task rather than as an important form of communication. During the 90/90/90 research, Dr. Reeves observed the writing portfolios in schools with high poverty and low achievement and found that student writing consisted of low-rigor writing tasks, such as acrostic poetry, and that nonfiction writing was nearly nonexistent.[2] This makes sense when we understand the trepidation that writing instruction conjures in both teachers and students.

Overcoming the struggles with writing instruction and achievement is worth the time and effort because, as evidenced in Dr. Reeves's 90/90/90 research, there is a clear correlation between the frequency of nonfiction writing and proficiency in math, science, reading, and social studies. When we talk about focusing on high-leverage strategies, writing is the bullseye in the center of the target.

Aligning Expectations and Preparing for Instruction

The first step to capitalizing on the power of nonfiction writing is understanding expectations and alignment throughout CLTs, grade levels, and departments.

- This can be a whole school initiative, but it could start with just one team as a grassroots effort.

FEARLESS INSTRUCTION

- Collaborating in teacher teams is a win-win when it comes to writing because teachers can strengthen their skills and their confidence with writing instruction and align expectations at the same time.
- Spending time developing an understanding of the finish line and starting line for students will pay off dividends with their achievement. John Hattie's research notes that "accurate estimates of student achievement" have a strong positive correlation with student achievement, as does teacher clarity.³

> **PRO TIP**
>
> It is okay to focus just on informational writing right now, and then after working through all four steps with nonfiction, you can circle back to the same process for the other genres of writing, such as opinion/argumentative and narrative.

The following four steps will support teacher teams with clarity and estimates of student achievement.

THE HOW

Understand the Finish Line

What are we looking for in student writing across grade levels?

It is important to start with a discussion about teacher perceptions of student writing. What are they currently looking for in their student writing? What successes and challenges are they finding? This discussion can help reveal what each teacher's finish line for writing is, or the skills they are hoping students develop by the end of the year. Chances are that the writing finish line varies from classroom to classroom, even within the same grade level.

What do our state standards say, and how are they scaffolded from year to year?

The state standards give us important insight into grade-level writing expectations and how they build on each other from year to year. It is helpful to look at the progression of standards in a table to help delineate the concepts and skills embedded in each standard.

Typical nonfiction writing standards for kindergarten through third grade and the required concepts and skills:

GRADE	NONFICTION WRITING STANDARD	ALIGNED SKILLS	CONCEPTS
Kindergarten	WK.2 Use a combination of drawing, dictating, and writing to compose informative/explanatory texts in which they name what they are writing about and supply some information about the topic.	Drawing, dictating, writing, naming topic, supplying information	Understanding topic expression through multiple modalities; basic content connection
1st Grade	W1.2 Write informative/explanatory texts in which they name a topic, supply some facts about the topic, and provide some sense of closure.	Naming topic, supplying facts, providing closure	Identifying key facts; understanding topic focus and closure
2nd Grade	W2.2 Write informative/explanatory texts in which they introduce a topic, use facts and definitions to develop points, and provide a concluding statement or section.	Introducing topic, using facts and definitions, including a concluding statement	Building informational structure; using definitions and factual support
3rd Grade	W3.2 Write informative/ explanatory texts to examine a topic and convey ideas and information clearly. a. Introduce a topic and group related information together; include illustrations when useful to aiding comprehension. b. Develop the topic with facts, definitions, and details. c. Use linking words and phrases (e.g., *also, another, and, more, but*) to connect ideas within categories of information. d. Provide a concluding statement or section.	Introducing and grouping related information, adding illustrations, developing with facts and details, using linking words, providing conclusion	Organizing information; cohesion with linking words; clarity and elaboration

FEARLESS INSTRUCTION

How do the standards translate into application on high-stakes assessments?
Utilizing released sample items from your state assessment to understand how the concepts and skills in the standards are applied on the assessment will give great insight into what students are expected to do independently by spring of each school year. This is an important component of developing an understanding of the rigor of the grade-level expectations and how students will be assessed.

How do our curriculum resources align with the standards, and which ones will help us get the best results?
Not everything is created equal when it comes to writing instruction, and sometimes the writing that is included in our core reading curriculum resources does not have the frequency or rigor that is necessary to scaffold students to independent application of the writing standards. In other words, our curriculum resources may not be enough to get students to the writing finish line. Or, sometimes there are resources like ELA performance tasks embedded into our reading curriculum that provide excellent instruction but are not used systematically.

Understand the Starting Line

What is the current state of writing achievement in our school?
There is a plethora of data to help us understand what the current strengths and weaknesses are with student writing. Target reports from state assessments and district benchmarks can provide valuable insights and help us understand where our students are succeeding and struggling. Classroom or school assessments allow teachers to look at actual student work to identify strengths and areas for growth. Are they able to analyze the prompt, or do the results indicate that many students score zero because they do not understand the prompt or read it carefully enough? Do the scores indicate that students have a strength or weakness in organization, elaboration, grammar, or conventions?

Where are pockets of excellence in our school when it comes to writing achievement?
Using achievement data and classroom work samples to help home in on pockets of excellence within your own school provides valuable information about how to optimize your curriculum resources, pacing guide, and schedule to improve student writing achievement. Often the experts are the teachers next door and learning from them is more valuable than any other professional learning.

Develop Grade-Level Rubrics

How will we assess proficiency from grade to grade?
The next step is to develop teacher-friendly and student-friendly writing rubrics that clearly outline the expectations for student writing. CLTs do not need to start from scratch with this as there are rubrics to guide writing expectations on state

assessments and within curriculum resources that can serve as guides. These can be adopted as-is or modified based on your particular context. The important part is that the rubrics set students up for success based on high expectations for their writing achievement, with the ultimate goal being that students can independently demonstrate the grade-level writing standards.

Developing clarity about the teachers' nonnegotiables is an important part of the process. Rubrics cannot be aligned with standards until there is a shared understanding of the concepts and skills in the curriculum expectations.

Tips for developing or selecting rubrics:

- **ALIGN ALL WRITING EXPECTATIONS WITH GRADE-LEVEL STANDARDS.** Teacher expectations should match what students are expected to do on high-stakes assessments and in the curriculum.
- **INCLUDE EVIDENCE, ELABORATION, AND ORGANIZATION AS PRIMARY INSTRUCTIONAL FOCUSES.** These areas typically make up 80% of writing scores and should be emphasized over mechanics alone.
- **EXPLICITLY TEACH AND REINFORCE GRADE-LEVEL APPROPRIATE GRAMMAR AND CONVENTIONS.** While not the primary focus, grammar and conventions are still essential to clear communication.
- **EMBED NONNEGOTIABLES DIRECTLY INTO STUDENT RUBRICS.** Rubrics should clearly outline what is expected so students can take ownership of their learning and teachers can provide consistent feedback.
- **USE WRITING INSTRUCTION TIME INTENTIONALLY.** Prioritize tasks and feedback that align with the most heavily weighted aspects of the writing standards.

> "The gold standard in rubric design is whether students can use the rubric to evaluate their own work and, as a result of this self-evaluation, reflect on and improve the quality of their work without waiting for the teacher's judgment."
>
> —DOUGLAS REEVES

The three-column rubric, introduced in Chapter 6, is a great tool to use to score and provide feedback to students on writing. It streamlines feedback and empowers students to understand expectations clearly, reflect on their progress, and take greater responsibility for their learning. This form of self-reflection and feedback helps students better understand expectations and saves teachers time by not having to comment on every part of the rubric.

Develop a Writing Action Plan

What steps will we take as a school to improve writing outcomes for all students?
Every step of this journey to improve writing achievement is exciting, but developing an action plan is where the rubber hits the road. Teacher teams get to take all that they have learned about writing expectations and achievement up to this point and develop a cohesive, actionable, and attainable plan. And, for those of us passionate about student success, this just might be the most exciting part of the work.

Sample instructional action plan for writing:

	EXPLANATORY WRITING	DATES
Step 1	Model the writing process with common strategies, including explicit instruction of rubric.	
Step 2	Guide practice with step-by-step, immediate feedback based on the rubric.	
Step 3	Have students complete independent writing (assessment at the end of the writing unit is not teacher-supported).	
Step 4	Align and calibrate scoring in CLT meetings; look for strengths and next steps.	
Step 5	Adjust instruction based on student needs; include small groups for intervention and extension.	

How quickly can we cycle through the writing action plan?
CLTs will determine the dates associated with each step based on the needs of their students.

- For younger grade levels, and especially those who have not been consistent with writing instruction and expectations, the steps may take longer. The entire process may take two to three weeks.
- For older grade levels who have higher writing achievement, students should eventually be able to work through the writing process in a week or less.
- It is important that teachers share effective writing instructional strategies with each other throughout the process. The best professional learning often comes from the teacher next door.

What steps will ensure our expectations are common?
Any rubric is a best-laid plan until it is put to the test with collaborative scoring. Bringing a class set of student writing and sorting their work into 1s, 2s, 3s, and 4s allows teachers to share the reasons

for the scores and talk about next instructional steps at the same time. (See Chapter 6 for more about collaborative scoring.)

THE WHAT

What Students Need: Classroom Writing Strategies for Motivation

Just as we have explored the crucial role of nonfiction writing in enhancing student achievement, it is equally important to recognize that motivation is the heartbeat of effective writing instruction. When students feel engaged and inspired, they are more likely to embrace writing as a meaningful form of communication rather than a burdensome task.

One fourth grade teacher team was surprised to discover that students could construct coherent paragraphs once they were given the chance to write to high school pen pals. The students cared deeply about their communication and how they were perceived by their high school role models, and this motivation was evident in their writing achievement. Their experience highlights the power of authentic connections in driving student engagement and growth in writing skills. As Dr. Reeves says, "We should think of writing as *thinking through the end of a pen*."[4] When students have an authentic purpose for their writing, it also reinforces that writing is not a task, it is a form of communication.

By fostering a motivating classroom environment, we can help students unlock their potential and view writing as an empowering tool for self-expression. The following strategies are designed to cultivate that motivation, ensuring that every student can thrive as a writer.

Suggested motivational writing practices:

PRACTICE	APPLICATION	MOTIVATION TIPS
ENGAGE WITH AUTHENTIC AUDIENCES	Provide real-world writing tasks with meaningful recipients (e.g., pen pals, community members).	Students care more when writing serves a real purpose and audience, increasing effort and engagement.
INCORPORATE SOCIAL-EMOTIONAL LEARNING	Integrate social-emotional learning skill practice into academic tasks, followed by written reflection on the experience.	Connecting academic content to personal growth makes learning more relevant and empowering.
PUBLISH STUDENT WRITING	Let students publish final drafts as individual or class books and share their work with peers, other grades, or families.	Publishing boosts pride and reinforces writing as a real, valued accomplishment.

CONNECT WRITING TO INTERESTS	Allow students to choose topics tied to personal interests like sports, music, or hobbies.	Interest-driven writing increases investment and enjoyment in the process.
USE MULTIMEDIA AND CHOICE	Offer options like podcast scripts, comics, or videos alongside traditional essays.	Creative formats invite personal expression and validate diverse communication styles.
LET STUDENTS BE THE TEACHERS	Flip the script and allow students to become the teachers. Writing is a tool to help them organize their thoughts and plan their lessons.	Reciprocal teaching is both engaging and effective—students deepen their own understanding by teaching others, while peer learning enhances comprehension for everyone.

ACTION STEPS

As educators, we have the opportunity to remove barriers and foster a culture of achievement that amplifies student voices and unlocks their potential. Follow these action steps to move students from fear to fire, helping them see writing as a powerful tool for communication, exploration, and lifelong success.

- ❏ Establish high expectations and align instruction
  - Collaboratively define what high-quality student writing looks like at each grade level.
  - Use writing standards and assessment rubrics to clarify expectations and align them across classrooms and grade levels.
- ❏ Make nonfiction writing a daily practice
  - Integrate nonfiction writing regularly across content areas, not just during ELA.
  - Use genres like explanatory, opinion, biographical, procedural, and reflective writing to build versatility and depth.
- ❏ Use student-friendly rubrics to support self-reflection
  - Develop or adapt 3-column rubrics that include success criteria, student self-assessment, and teacher feedback.
  - Empower students to monitor their own growth and reduce teacher workload by only responding where feedback diverges.
- ❏ Create motivating, real-world writing experiences
  - Provide authentic audiences (e.g., pen pals, community members) and publish student work.
  - Incorporate social-emotional reflection, student choice, and multimedia formats to increase relevance and motivation.
- ❏ Implement collaborative scoring and instructional cycles
  - Facilitate regular team meetings to calibrate scoring, analyze writing samples, and adjust instruction based on student needs.
  - Use short, flexible writing cycles (2 to 3 weeks for younger students, 1 week for advanced writers) with a clear progression: model, guided practice, independent writing, reflection, and reteaching.

NONFICTION WRITING

Aligning Expectations and Preparing for Instruction

Understand the Finish Line
- What are we looking for in student writing across grade levels?
- What do our state standards say?
- How are they scaffolded from year to year?
- How are they assessed?

Understand the Starting Line
- What is the current state of writing achievement in our school?
- Where are pockets of excellence in our school when it comes to writing achievement?

Develop Grade-Level Rubrics
- How will we assess proficiency from grade to grade?
- What are the nonnegotiables across all grades?
- Can students use the rubric to evaluate their own work without waiting on teacher input?

Develop a Writing Action Plan
- What actions will we take as a school to improve writing outcomes for all students?
- How quickly can we cycle through the writing action plan?
- What steps will ensure our expectations are common?

 2025 Creative Leadership Press. This page may be reproduced for classroom use only. All other rights reserved.

FAST FEEDBACK FOUNDATIONS

BIG IDEAS
FEEDBACK
MULTIPLE OPPORTUNITIES
SPECIFIC
CONCEPTUAL UNDERSTANDING

THIS PIECE SHARPENS THE IMAGE—FEEDBACK BRINGS CLARITY TO LEARNING BY showing students where they are, where they're going, and how to get there." In this chapter, we explore the tenets of FAST (Fair, Accurate, Specific, and Timely) Feedback and how this type of feedback can improve performance at any level. In addition to learning about FAST Feedback, we review classroom scenarios and explore ways for teachers and instructional leaders to provide feedback to teachers and students to drive student learning.

Classrooms with high rates of feedback are the most engaging learning environments to enter. Teachers can be seen giving global feedback to their entire class through formative opportunities or individually as they walk around and monitor student progress using rubrics.

The educational system is filled with feedback. We provide feedback in areas of attendance, behavior, and meeting instructional learning targets. Our ability to give feedback to students is one of the most impactful ways to support the entire learning process. Among all forms of feedback, FAST Feedback, as coined by Dr. Douglas Reeves,[1] is one of the best ways to make sure that an educator's feedback to students is effective.

FAST Feedback should be

- efficient,
- meaningful, and
- in the moment, allowing the student to make immediate changes.

The end of this chapter includes a FAST Feedback guide to keep your skills sharp.

THE WHY

Setting the Stage for Feedback

In Ms. Blake's room, the learning standard progressions are posted for each secondary language arts course that she teaches, including ninth grade introductory courses and college level courses. When an entire class has mastered a content standard, it is added to a completion poster so they know it will be on future assessments. Global feedback shows learners that they are collectively part of the learning process.

Let's highlight what is different in this classroom:
- Individual students can clearly articulate the standard they are working on and their next step in learning.
- Color-coded writing indicates student progress toward the standard, and students can explain the intentional purpose of each color.
- Notes are intentional learning tools, not an assignment or task, that students use as a resource to improve their conceptual understanding.
- Multiple learning tasks outlined on the board guide student learning toward meeting the standard.
- Multiple assignments are being worked on because student feedback is used to plan lessons that are designed to move all learners forward.

To the casual eye, this may seem chaotic, but to the trained educator, this is differentiated instruction based on feedback and is a model of student learning.

FEARLESS INSTRUCTION

Low expectations due to poverty, language needs, disabilities, or advanced courses can become a justification for a lack of high-quality instruction and feedback. These reasons could not be more wrong. All learners have the right to receive high-quality feedback and instruction daily. Equitable outcomes can only happen when these features are found in all levels of academic offerings in a school.

Imagine the immediate improvement students could make in the classroom and across contents if the entire educational system followed the FAST mindset, providing fair, accurate, specific, and timely feedback. Academic achievement improves by taking the focus off final grades and placing the importance on the actual learning. Fearless instruction coupled with feedback makes real learning happen for educators and students alike.

THE HOW

All learners thrive on feedback. When educators misconstrue grades for feedback, they lose an opportunity to help students grow their conceptual understanding and achieve at higher levels. Feedback that is fair, accurate, specific, and timely removes ambiguity and values both the time of the teacher who is providing feedback and the student who has a goal of demonstrating proficiency on their path to graduation. The ongoing use of formative assessments, rubrics, and allowing for revisions enhances the learning environment and makes it equitable for all learners.

High-Quality Feedback in Action

This 6th grade daily math review is an excellent model of FAST Feedback. The Math Review process is a structured mathematical concept review that allows work time, collaboration time, teacher feedback, and reflection.[2] All students in the room work on the same problems with a challenge question at the end. Students are presented with a previously taught but not yet mastered concept.

- Students start by reviewing their notes and independently solve the problems.
- Following individual time, students work with a partner and use specific problem-solving sentence stems to explain their thinking and support each other in correcting any misconceptions.
- Collaboration and correction are followed by the teacher solving the problem by using direct instruction, highlighting misconceptions, and giving students time to correct their own work in the moment.
- After all students have the correct answer, they are given time to reflect on their work by using specific mathematical vocabulary.

The entire exercise takes no more than 15 minutes and provides specific and timely feedback to the teacher and students in the class. Students take a short assessment on the specific concepts reviewed at the end of the week to help the teacher plan the following week's review.

Quality feedback is not just for students; it should be modeled at all levels. Leaders have an important role to play in the process of giving FAST Feedback. They should not only be reviewing feedback given to students and asking students questions about their task progression when visiting classrooms, but they should also set the same example with educators in their school and district.

Educators are learners, too, and all learners deserve high-quality feedback that is fair, accurate, specific, and timely. Teacher observations should be partnered with feedback that will help them improve their practice. Teachers should know exactly what the observer expects when they enter the classroom and how they should perform to meet those expectations. In our last example, let's explore what FAST Feeback provided to teachers can look like.

FAST Feedback for Teachers from Leaders

Let's consider an example of a superintendent who visits classrooms in her district on a regular basis. In her visits, she leaves a sticky note for the educator to appreciate something she observes or hears while in the classroom. These are written clearly as notes of appreciation and not guidelines for instructional improvement. However, when the observation relates to a district priority, the feedback is far more specific.

Examples of specific sticky note feedback:
- I appreciate your use of sentence frames with students and that ALL students were on task.
- I noticed that the learning targets were articulated on the board.
- The three students I spoke with shared their next steps in the progression.

These feedback notes are left in all grade levels, as district level literacy and instructional expectations are the same K–12. If the superintendent began leaving notes that discussed bulletin board quality or classroom seating arrangements, it would be unfair as these priorities have not been articulated at a district level.

When leaders use observations solely to evaluate, they miss the opportunity to coach teachers and to provide valuable instructional direction to improve performance. Waiting days for feedback from an evaluator can cause unnecessary anxiety and impacts trust. And when that feedback lacks next steps, it can be overwhelming and useless. We learn best in a psychologically safe environment,[3] and providing

FAST Feedback sets the stage to help the entire organization learn and should be followed by the leader. As Dr. Reeves says, people aren't evaluated into better performance, they are coached into it.

Now that you have explored how FAST Feedback is put into action, let's explore what it means to fill your classroom with rich feedback that leads to improvement.

THE WHAT

Providing FAST Feedback to Students

Fair

"But it isn't fair." How often have we heard that things aren't fair? Understanding what students need and why is important for both the teacher and the student to be successful. It also sets the stage for an equal playing field of learning. On the playground, in the lunchroom, and in the classroom, fairness is debated by students and sometimes even parents. Where the debate should never happen, though, is in our feedback.

Students have the right to know that how they are graded is not a secret. Fairness directly relates to educator clarity, and this clarity allows students to become active participants in their own learning progression.[4] Educators must be consistent across the department and school, with clear expectations for both what students need to do now and where they are headed next in their learning. This clarity is vital to ensure that the feedback is equitable for all. (See Chapter 6 for more on teacher clarity.)

Whether emerging or advanced, all students deserve to know and understand exactly what they are learning and where they are going in their next steps.[5] Without this clarity of expectations, students can feel lost and lack connection to the task at hand. What do we do when we feel lost? Sadly, we often give up. It is the educator's job to fill the gap so expectations are clear and feedback is fair and consistent for all learners.

Fair Feedback in Action

- State expectations clearly, grounded in learning intentions and success criteria.
- Use consistent expectations across grade levels and content areas.
- Ensure students know where they're headed by sharing next steps in learning.

Accurate

Accurate feedback is based on the standards, learning goals, and success criteria that were specified in the task and learning progression.[6] When educators assign a task to a student and then grade it or provide feedback on additional expectations, the lack of accuracy on the grade can be frustrating for the student and also lead to false reporting of student ability. Students should know precisely what they need to do to meet the standard, how they met the standards, and what they need to do next to improve. Using scoring guides and rubrics are simple ways to provide accurate feedback. (See Chapter 6 for more details on scoring guides and rubrics.)

When educators add expectations that have not been clearly communicated to the student, accuracy can go south quickly. Consider a math assignment that is focused on problem-solving where a student receives a low grade, not because the solution is incorrect, but because of spelling and grammar. Although precise communication is part of the standards for mathematical practice, the grade should reflect the student's ability to solve the problem. Spelling and grammar are important, but if the grade only reflects the mathematical practice and not the ability to solve the problem, it is not accurate.

Accurate Feedback in Action

- Base feedback on established criteria. Use evidence from the student work to support your feedback.
- Align feedback and grades to reflect performance on the assigned content or academic standards.
- Ensure students understand the feedback and would agree based on the clarity of expectations.

Specific

When providing specific feedback using established success criteria, the educator shows the student where they are in the learning progression. This feedback guides students on what steps to take next to become proficient or to exceed the standard. Specific feedback outlines the road map for student growth and allows all students to achieve. Feedback that lacks next steps for improvement is only a report of learning and not a path to improvement.

When students have a clear path for improvement, their learning becomes more personal. It also helps educators plan focused mini-lessons for all learners, including those ready for advanced work. Specific feedback can be found by asking students two questions: "What are we doing? What are we doing next?"[7] When students can answer these two questions, you know you are in a classroom that thrives on feedback.

FAST FEEDBACK

⚖️ Fair

- State expectations clearly, grounded in learning intentions and success criteria.
- Use consistent expectations across grade levels and content areas.
- Ensure students see where they're headed by sharing the next steps in learning.

🎯 Accurate

- Base feedback on established criteria. Use evidence from the student work to support your feedback.
- Align feedback and grades to reflect performance on the assigned content or academic standards.
- Ensure students understand the feedback and would agree based on the clarity of expectations.

📝 Specific

- Provide concrete, measurable steps for improvement so all students can progress.
- Let students know what they are doing and where they are going next.
- Ensure students know and can verbalize their own steps for improvement.

📋 Timely

- Provide feedback in the moment or as close to the misconception as possible by using sticky notes, student conferencing, whisper coaching, etc.
- Use quick formative checks or have students use their rubric to check off expectations during work time.
- Ensure students have time to reflect, adjust their learning, and ask for help as needed.

Specific Feedback in Action

- Provide concrete, measurable steps for improvement so all students can progress.
- Let students know what they are doing and where they are going next.
- Ensure students know and can verbalize their own steps for improvement.

Timely

There is nothing more frustrating for students or adults than to spend their time on an assignment or task and then wait for days or even weeks to get feedback. Timely feedback keeps students engaged in their learning progression. At the point there is a gap between completion and feedback and no opportunity to reflect, continue learning, and revise, then the learning is lost.

Feedback provided in the moment not only enhances the learning environment with ongoing feedback and opportunity, but it provides a connection to the work that the students may not otherwise have. Another way to think of the importance of timely feedback is this: Educators spend countless hours assessing student work, writing in the margins, and demonstrating their knowledge of the content. When students don't have the time or expectation to reflect on the work, get instructional assistance, and revise, all that learning is held by the teacher and the student's involvement is passive, at best.[8]

Timely Feedback in Action

- Provide feedback in the moment or as close to the misconception as possible by using sticky notes, student conferencing, whisper coaching, etc.
- Use quick formative checks or have students use their rubric to check off expectations during work time.
- Ensure students have time to reflect, adjust their learning, and ask for help as needed.

ACTION STEPS

- ❏ Analyze recent feedback you have given your students to ensure your feedback matches the identified learning targets and standards.
- ❏ Ask your students two questions: What are you doing? Where are you going next?
- ❏ Develop a system of frequency in your feedback to support timely feedback with the opportunity to continue learning and revise.

SECTION II REVIEW

Throughout this section, we explored the key components of rigor, fair and accurate grading, clarity, rubrics, nonfiction writing, and FAST Feedback to facilitate fearless instruction in classrooms.

- In Chapter 5, we examined the stages of learning and how teams can use the Hess Cognitive Rigor Matrix to evaluate their standards, assignments, and assessments. Understanding the role of rigor helps teams create clear criteria to engage in fair and accurate feedback and grading.

- In Chapter 6, we applied our understanding of rigor to create clarity in expectations through the development of learning intentions and success criteria. Implementing these tools leads to clarity and the creation of student-friendly rubrics. These powerful and clear rubrics lay the groundwork for calibration through collaborative scoring.

- In Chapter 7, we reviewed the power of nonfiction writing and its potential to motivate all students. We presented the steps your teams can take to create action and implementation plans for nonfiction writing at your school.

- In Chapter 8, we brought the pieces in this section together to create the conditions for providing FAST Feedback. Learning to use actionable feedback at all levels sets your school on the path for continued improvement.

REFLECTION QUESTIONS

- ❑ Think about a time you were learning a new skill or concept. How did you know when you "got it"?
- ❑ How can learning intentions and success criteria be used with students as part of daily classroom instruction?
- ❑ What benefits do you see for using rubrics to collaboratively score student work with your peers? What are the benefits of having students use rubrics to peer assess?
- ❑ Why might teachers feel intimidated by writing instruction, and what strategies could help build their confidence and effectiveness in teaching nonfiction writing?
- ❑ How do you use student feedback on classroom work to drive your instructional decision-making?
- ❑ How is your feedback to students reflected in your instruction?

— SECTION III —
FINISHING THE PUZZLE
Engaging Everyone

LITERACY
A Team Sport

BIG IDEAS
READING ACQUISITION
HIGH-QUALITY TEXTS
DISCUSSION
VOCABULARY

THIS CHAPTER ADDS A CENTER PIECE. LITERACY CONNECTS ALL THE OTHER PIECES, bridging language to learning across every subject and strategy. In this chapter, we discuss the playbook for developing literacy at every level and explore strategies for all content and elective area teachers to develop literacy in their students. First, we parse the difference between learning to read and reading to learn, and then we explore what teachers need to be effective coaches of literacy, including shared instructional agreements and high-quality, diverse texts. We finish the chapter by delving into effective research-based practices that bolster students' reading comprehension: reading, writing, and discussion protocols and explicit vocabulary instruction.

LITERACY

While there is widespread consensus on the value of being a proficient reader and writer in schools and society today, there is a fundamental lack of clarity on how *all* teachers contribute to creating highly literate students, especially after elementary school. You may have heard the saying that students in kindergarten through third grade are *learning to read* and students in grades 4–12 *reading to learn*. But this common saying is misleading because every teacher has a role to play.

Students deserve direct instruction in the language of every content area as well as the opportunity to read, write, and discuss concepts and terms in authentic texts in every classroom. They need meaningful engagement with text, explicit vocabulary instruction, and consistent opportunities to discuss concepts and ideas within and beyond the classroom.

This chapter includes a note catcher to help you and your team capture notes and ideas on the intricate process of moving from learning to read to reading to learn as you read this chapter. The chapter also includes explicit vocabulary instruction strategies and a template to use to create an action plan for developing literacy-rich classrooms.

> **Making meaning, developing fluency, acquiring vocabulary, and comprehending language draw from both learning to read and reading to learn skills. Both are necessary for our students to become proficient readers.**

THE WHY

Students are engaged in an infinity loop of learning to read and reading to learn, and all teachers contribute to the development of literacy through the deliberate expansion of students' background knowledge, vocabulary acquisition, critical thinking skills, and understanding of language and text structures. As students gain vocabulary and experience with texts and ideas, they become better readers.

We know that students need to read frequently and widely to become better readers. In a nationally normed assessment,[1] students in fifth grade who read 65 minutes a day outside of school encountered over 4 million words. In contrast, students who read an average of 4.6 minutes a day outside of school encountered 282,000 words and ranked at 50%. A student in the first group read 14 times the number of words as a student in the second group.

DEVELOPING LITERACY AT EVERY LEVEL

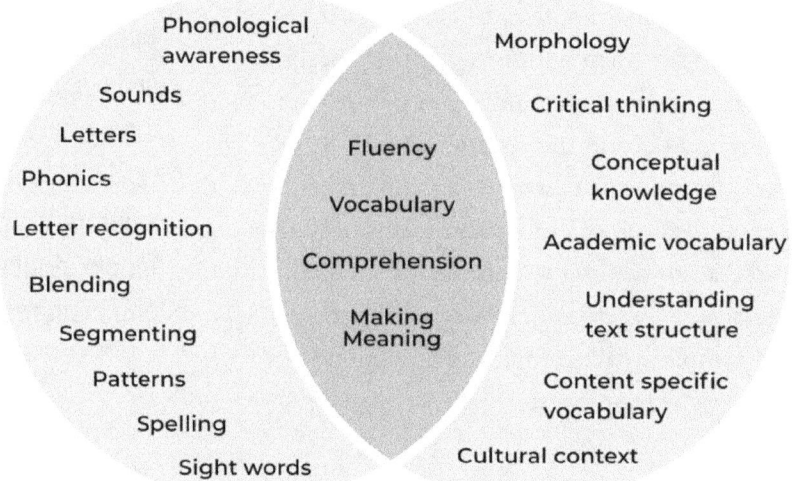

User this note catcher to capture ideas on the intricate process of moving from learning to read to reading to learn.

Learning to Read—Aquiring Language	Reading to Learn—Acquiring Knowledge

Relationship between time spent reading and words read per year:

PERCENT	INDEPENDENT READING MINUTES PER DAY	WORDS READ PER YEAR
98%	65	4,358,000
90%	21.1	1,823,000
80%	14.2	1,146,000
70%	9.6	622,000
60%	6.5	432,000
50%	4.6	282,000
40%	3.2	200,000
30%	1.3	106,000
20%	0.7	21,000
10%	0.1	8,000
2%	0	0

The findings here have two major implications. First, students should read widely in all subject areas and should have time to discuss and construct knowledge from these texts. Lectures, notes, discussion protocols, and explicit vocabulary lessons are not a substitute for reading and processing ideas and word meanings in context. The second implication is that time spent reading within and beyond the classroom is imperative to building knowledgeable students.

To be a proficient reader in a specific discipline, whether it is history, music, or algebra, the reader needs to do the following:

- Be knowledgeable about concepts and ideas
- Use specialized vocabulary
- Interpret information, illustrations, charts, and graphs
- Navigate complex texts
- Understand the specific format, genre, and/or structure
- Consider the reliability of sources and the quality of evidence

These skills, among others, are the purview of all teachers. To empower students to be proficient readers and thinkers in multiple disciplines, all teachers must embrace their contributions to content acquisition and literacy development.

FEARLESS INSTRUCTION

THE HOW

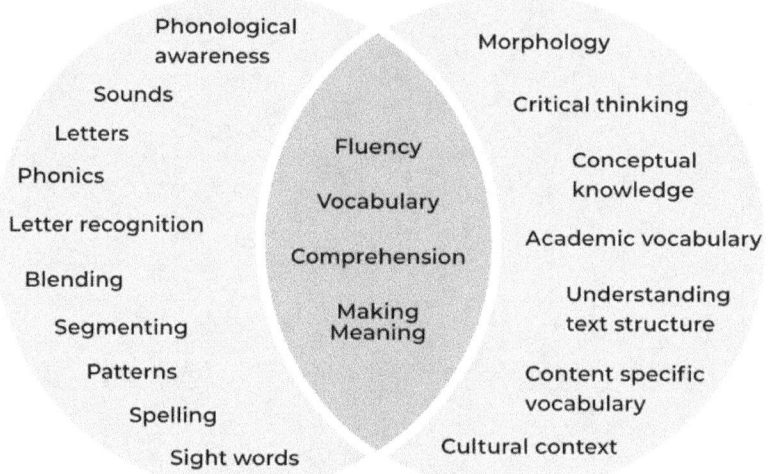

LEARNING TO READ: Acquiring Language

It is true that primary teachers teach students to read—specifically, to focus on word recognition and phonics—but this is only the beginning of competence in reading effectively.

Let's explore one popular model of reading acquisition so that we can understand how teachers of all grades and subjects contribute to developing skilled readers. The Simple View of Reading suggests that learning to read can be represented by a mathematical equation.[2]

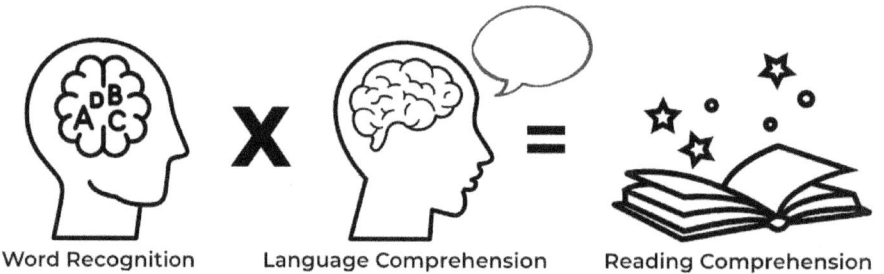

First, a student learns to decode or recognize words.
This entails systematic, explicit phonics instruction of 26 letters, 44 sounds or phonemes, and over 250 spellings or graphemes. Students learn how sound, pattern, and meaning work together in words.

- For example, a student learns that there are five short vowels *a*, *e*, *i*, *o*, and *u* and there are multiple ways to spell or read long vowels. The long *a* sound, for example, can be spelled as follows: *a* as in *table*, *ai* as in *rain*, *ay* as in *play*, *a-consonant-e* as in *cake*, *ei* as in *veil*, *eigh* as in *eight* and even *au* as in *gauge*.

Phonics and word recognition are the first part of the equation. This can be described as "lifting words off the page." Word recognition is necessary, but insufficient alone in learning to read effectively.

Then, a student builds language comprehension.
Primary teachers are often considered the experts in learning to read due to their knowledge of phonics, decoding, and early literacy skills, but there is a false assumption that once a student can read words, they can also comprehend the language.

- For example, take the word *supercalifragilisticexpialidocious*. Students with effective decoding skills can read all 34 letters and 14 syllables flawlessly. But unless they have had the experience of watching the movie *Mary Poppins*, they have no understanding of the word or its context.

Because language comprehension is influenced by background knowledge, language development, vocabulary, and reasoning, all content and elective teachers need to spend time incorporating literacy strategies so that students can fully engage with the material in their classes.

Finally, a student achieves comprehension.
Once a student can automatically recognize words, they must be able to assign meaning to the words and, eventually, phrases and paragraphs.

- For example, reading the words *petal*, *peddle*, and *pedal* requires not only an understanding of sound and pattern, but *meaning*. Consider how "The child was *pedaling* her bike" is different from "The florist was *peddling* flower arrangements at the market."

In our equation, if either word recognition or language comprehension is zero, then reading comprehension is zero. Students must be able to decode and recognize words accurately through the deliberate practice of phonics to understand the meaning of words, sentences, and phrases.

READING TO LEARN: Acquiring Knowledge

Shared Rules of the Game: Instructional Agreements
To deliver effective learning opportunities for students to learn content and develop literacy, teachers need a common set of rules for the game of learning. Grade levels and content departments need shared instructional agreements that include common research-based

> **PRO TIP**
> Five minutes of content reading in each class adds up to significant opportunities to learn vocabulary and knowledge.

practices such as reading and discussion protocols and explicit vocabulary instruction, as well as collections of engaging resources and text sets.

Sample shared instructional agreements for all content area teachers, including fine arts, physical education, and electives:

- Teach vocabulary twice a week with 3 to 5 evidence-based strategies.
- Provide a text-based lesson twice a week with a reading and discussion protocol to maximize engagement.

With agreements in place, teachers need common planning and reflection time. Common time focused on instructional planning and reflection is like watching the film of the game. Teachers are consistently adjusting their plans in response to student needs.

Questions to ask:

- To what degree are our instructional practices and formative assessment strategies working for our students?
- Do vocabulary assessments reflect success for all students or only some?
- What went well? Where should we adjust?

The Playing Field: Knowledge-Building Through High-Quality Text Sets

A common teaching method which persists in our classrooms today is for a teacher to provide information through lecture and then have students follow up with reading from and answering questions in the textbook.

Textbooks are known to be a mile wide and an inch deep; they cover too many concepts without delving into the varied human experiences and perspectives that provide an in-depth understanding of the subject area.

Textbooks are also notoriously written at a reading level that surpasses the age, grade, and development of their readers. While teachers can argue that these methods build knowledge, a more robust approach is possible.

> **PRO TIP**
> Text sets can start small by pairing two passages or texts.

The more robust approach includes the use of diverse text sets—collections of high-quality texts on the same topic that provide multiple perspectives, formats, and levels of complexity—to build knowledge. These collections may include picture books, novels, expository articles, and multimedia sources such as films, podcasts, videos, and TED Talks.

These rich and varied reading materials are critical to motivating students to develop knowledge in all content areas. With high-quality text sets, teachers in all classes can focus on the acquisition of vocabulary, experience, and conceptual knowledge in their content area. Texts by different authors and in different formats are not only more interesting and thought-provoking than textbooks, notes, and lectures, but the use of multiple texts also creates an opportunity for interdependence among readers.

Students read different texts and bring their unique contributions, facts, and experiences to the conversations. Students may also note that varied texts amplify some ideas and leave others out.

Strategies for curating collections of compelling text sets:

- Include picture books, novels, articles, podcasts, plays, poems, primary sources, and multimedia.
- Select multilevel and highly engaging texts.
- Incorporate visuals, graphs, illustrations, photographs, and infographics.
- Provide different entry points for students to engage with content.

A Text Set for the Great Migration

Let's consider a social studies teacher who is preparing to teach the Great Migration (1917–1970) when millions of African Americans moved from rural communities in the South to cities in the North to escape racial violence and to pursue economic opportunities.

Rather than lectures and notes, the teacher could provide the following rich text set and strategies:

- A TED Talk by Pulitzer Prize winner Isabel Wilkerson followed by guided discussion with their peers and independent, written reflection.
- Jigsaw groups where students read multiple sources, including excerpts and complete works, such as these:
    - *The Warmth of Other Suns* by Isabel Wilkerson
    - *South Side Girls* by Marcia Chatelain
    - *The Promised Land* by Nicholas Leman
    - *The Great Migration: A Play in Three Acts* by Acie Cargill

For younger readers, the following picture books are engaging:
- *This Is the Rope* by Jacqueline Woodson
- *The Great Migration: Journey to the North* by Eloise Greenfield
- *The Great Migration* by Jacob Lawrence

What Teachers Need from Leaders

In the next section, we discuss what leaders can do to sustain effective literacy instruction. They can do so by consistently monitoring progress and celebrating small successes, which build momentum.[3] This requires focus and action on a weekly basis. Leaders must intentionally observe the status of shared instructional agreements and reflect progress to staff during learning walks, in faculty meetings, and via weekly newsletters. Acknowledgement of and appreciation for the craft is invaluable, as is candor and reflection on the results.

> **Ideas to help leaders monitor and celebrate growth:**
>
> - Count the number of discussion protocols implemented in a week or the amount of time students spend reading or writing in each class each day.
> - Consider having teachers self-report the number of discussion protocols or vocabulary strategies used in a week.
> - Share the data across content areas.
> - Highlight successes across classrooms with formative assessments.

THE WHAT

What Students Need

In the literacy game, teachers and students are engaged in a series of well-coordinated instructional moves, actions, or *plays* with one another, with their teammates, and with content resources. To be effective readers and learners, students need research-based practices that support their learning:

1. **Reading, writing, and discussion protocols.** A set of guidelines for conversations to ensure that all students are engaged with content and one another.
2. **Explicit vocabulary instruction.**

Joining the Game: Reading, Writing, And Discussion Protocols

Engagement with content and peers is important for every child. According to John Hattie's meta-analysis of factors affecting student learning,[4] classroom discussion earns an effect size of .82, which means that classroom discussions earn twice the average effect. In short, students learn more when they talk about the content. (See the introduction for a recap of Hattie's work on effect sizes.)

Even more compelling than traditional classroom discussion, the specific use of the Jigsaw method earns an effect size of 1.2. During a Jigsaw routine, students are responsible for reading and teaching the main points to their peer group. Students are engaged in the content, and teachers are coaching the discussion. As an example, students could be assigned to one of five different resources about the Great Migration. Expert groups would read, discuss, and take notes from one source and then be reassigned to a mixed group (one person from each text or source group) to share what they learned and to learn from four other peers and resources. This routine engages students with one text deeply and creates interdependence among learners, expanding what is understood.

Another protocol is the simple use of partnerships and a "Read and Say Something" or Think–Pair–Share instructional routine. Students are partnered to read portions of the text and then to "say something" about what they understood or thought. This simple protocol increases comprehension and processing.

Reading, writing, and discussion protocols are the skills of the sport, the instructional moves of the classroom. Whether teachers teach fourth grade, orchestra, or microbiology, their instructional routines determine whether students have the opportunity to engage in conversation or sit passively on the sidelines.

Calling the Plays: Explicit Vocabulary Instruction

It has been said that students in middle school need a passport to move from period to period, as each teacher and each subject have individual rules around behavior, grading, instructional practices, language, and vocabulary. If literacy is to be a team sport, we want our teachers and students playing the same game, on the same field, and with the same high-leverage strategies across the content areas, which includes the development of vocabulary.

> Text is the single most influential source of vocabulary.
> ⌄
> Students who read widely have rich vocabularies.
> ⌄
> Strong vocabulary is correlated with better comprehension.
> ⌄
> Teachers have the power to immerse students in a multitude of texts.

Students who read widely have a rich vocabulary, and strong vocabulary is correlated with strong comprehension. Research shows that students need both direct and indirect instruction in vocabulary.[5] There are several research-based strategies to effectively teach vocabulary. These direct strategies for vocabulary development should also be coupled with reading the words in an authentic context, increasing the exposure, breadth, and depth of word meanings.

Research-based instructional strategies to teach vocabulary:

VOCABULARY STRATEGIES	DEFINITIONS
Concept Mapping	A concept map is a type of graphic organizer used to help students organize and represent knowledge of a subject. The map is a visual depiction of how concepts and vocabulary are related to one another. They are focused on one key concept.
Frayer Model[6]	The Frayer model is a type of graphic organizer that includes a word's definition, facts and characteristics of the word, and examples and non-examples. It was designed to demonstrate deep understanding about a single word.
List–Group–Label	List–Group–Label (LGL) is a semantic map strategy that helps students organize concepts, improve their vocabulary, and develop categorization skills. It's an interactive, critical thinking strategy that can be used before or after students read to help them recognize relationships between words and concepts using their prior knowledge. • List terms and phrases from a single area of study. • Sort or categorize the words and discuss thinking for the categorization. • Create a label for each group.
Morphological Analysis[7]	A strategy to systematically break apart words to consider the meaning. Examine the word for meaningful parts—base word, prefixes, or suffixes. • Find the base word by removing a prefix or suffix. • Look at the base to see if you know it or if you can think of a related word (a word that has the same base). • Reassemble the word, thinking about the meaning contributed by the base, the suffix, and then the prefix. This should give you a more specific idea of what the word is. • Try out the meaning in the sentence; check if it makes sense in the context of the sentence and the larger context of the text that is being read. • If the word still does not make sense and is critical to the meaning of the overall passage, look it up in the dictionary.

LITERACY

ACTION STEPS

Leaders, you have the responsibility to connect how students learn to read to the instructional practices in the building. Collaborative Learning Teams, you have the responsibility to agree on common instructional moves.

All students deserve

- access to varied, highly engaging text sets;
- the use of structured protocols for reading, writing, and discussion; and,
- routines for explicit vocabulary instruction.

All teachers need

- professional learning and time with one another to curate materials,
- agreements on high-leverage teaching strategies, and
- time for reflection.

Educational administrators should

- ensure that teachers have robust resources,
- design instructional schedules that promote collaboration and adaptation,
- monitor teaching and learning and the shared instructional agreements and the response of the students, and
- celebrate progress and build collective accountability.

DEVELOPING LITERACY IN ALL CLASSROOMS

Work with your team to develop an action plan for each key component to a literacy-rich classroom.

Key Component	Team Action Plan
Instructional Agreements	
High-Quality Text Sets	
Discussion Protocols	
Vocabulary Strategies	

BIG IDEAS
CURRICULAR CONNECTIONS
CROSSCUTTING CONCEPTS
SOCIAL-EMOTIONAL LEARNING

CROSS-DISCIPLINARY INTEGRATION
More Brains Are Better Than One

HERE, WE FILL IN THE MIDDLE WITH A STRATEGY THAT BRINGS CONTENT areas and the learner closer together. In this chapter, we explore how CLTs can take their planning to the next level with cross-disciplinary teaching. We discuss how teams at the beginning of cross-disciplinary teaching and learning can start by finding crosscutting ideas in content areas and planning units together. If teams have been engaging with cross-disciplinary work and are looking to rejuvenate practices, social-emotional learning competencies can be embedded into daily instruction. Finally, a cross-disciplinary team planning template is included at the end of this chapter.

In 1916, John Dewey had a vision for students. His New Education called for educators to remain flexible to student needs, to help students learn more than just lessons to better understand the life of their community, and to develop the capacity to adapt to social needs.[1] While it was not called cross-disciplinary teaching or social-emotional learning, his vision spelled out how it would help students then and now.

When educators engage in cross-disciplinary planning they collaborate to align skills among subject areas to maximize the benefits of connected curriculum and assessments. When educators focus on the process of cross-disciplinary teaching, they provide deeper learning, real-world application, and assessment through performance tasks.

From Dewey all the way through the Common Core State Standards, cross-disciplinary teaching has been a part of the conversation. Similarly, the noted importance of social-emotional competencies has also been critical to student success. The question becomes how to pull the two together to make the most of learning for students. Using both the CLT structure and an interdisciplinary team structure, educators can bring together the benefits of focus and collaboration to create curricular and social connections for students.

Let's Explore
CROSS-DISCIPLINARY LEARNING
A Walk Through History

WHOLE CHILD — **1916**
John Dewey published *Democracy and Education* urging educators to consider the whole child, not treat them as empty vessels.

SOCIAL-EMOTIONAL LEARNING — **1994**
The Collaborative for Academic, Social, and Emotional Learning (CASEL) introduced the original social-emotional learning competencies.

90/90/90 RESEARCH — **1995**
In the 90/90/90 research, Dr. Douglas Reeves et al. found that cross-disciplinary integration increased engagement and student performance, deeming it a high-leverage strategy.

TURNING POINTS 2000 — **2000**
Carnegie Corporation published its findings and recommended integrated curriculum and cross-disciplinary planning as best practices for middle-level education.

SEL ADOPTION — **2002**
27 states adopted K–12 Social-Emotional Learning competencies.

90/90/90 RESEARCH UPDATE — **2003**
Original research was updated, stating that cross-disciplinary teaching should be expanded to include all subject areas to improve results for students.

COMMON CORE — **2009**
Common Core State Standards (CCSS) were introduced, expanding cross-disciplinary approaches beyond the arts to include many more content areas.

CASEL UPDATE — **2022**
All 50 states adopted Pre-K social-emotional competencies with a greater emphasis on integrating these into daily instruction rather than treating as a stand-alone program.

NEA ENDORSEMENT — **2023**
The National Education Association (NEA) supported experience-based, cross-disciplinary teaching for both academics and social-emotional learning.

 2025 Creative Leadership Press. This page may be reproduced for classroom use only. All other rights reserved.

The end of this chapter includes a Cross-Disciplinary Planning Template that integrates social-emotional competencies with academic standards.

THE WHY

Just as literacy is for everyone, so too are the intentional connection of content areas and the inclusion of social-emotional learning. Students deserve to be educated in a way that connects their learning, provides relevance, and reinforces the importance of essential life skills.

Connect Learning

Cross-disciplinary teaching provides opportunities for students as they experience how content can be connected, resulting in making deeper meaning of the learning. When teachers intentionally connect the curriculum for students, they can activate multiple parts of the brain making learning more meaningful. When students make meaning of the content, they can move beyond surface learning to deep and transfer learning. For example, a student who is learning how to make an inference in reading can also apply those inferencing skills to graphs in science or math.

Reflecting on the demands placed on our older students, it's clear that cross-disciplinary learning isn't just an instructional strategy, it's a necessary shift. Intentionally connecting content across subjects reduces the cognitive overload caused by fragmented schedules and heavy course loads. In *How Julie's Brain Learns*, Eric Jensen highlights how learning can get lost in the shuffle of disconnected classes for a first-year high school student.

Traditional bell schedules that break the day into even parts where students see teachers every day often disrupt learning momentum with class changes happening every 42 to 45 minutes. Intentionally creating continuity across disciplines provides students with a more coherent and meaningful experience. That consistency not only deepens understanding but also lightens the cognitive load on the adolescent brain.

Provide Relevance

Cross-disciplinary teaching creates the conditions for hands-on, student-centered instruction. Interdisciplinary projects and performance tasks provide multiple opportunities to include real-world scenarios, which increases student voice and choice in the product. When multiple content areas come together to explore the same ideas from different perspectives, students have rich opportunities to reflect, form their own opinions, and deepen their understanding.

When educators engage in the process of cross-disciplinary planning, which Berckemeyer describes as "cooperating on curriculum,"[2] students reap the benefits of learning that is relevant and connected:

- Students who engage in cross-disciplinary learning see how big ideas show up in multiple disciplines.
- Students who participate in learning activities that are connected through "correlated instructional approaches"[3] have greater ownership over their learning.

To increase relevancy and strengthen connections across curriculum, teachers can most effectively assess performance tasks and projects by using rubrics. (See Chapter 6 for more on rubrics.) In interdisciplinary teams, teachers collaborate to build rubrics with clearly defined success criteria, thereby creating meaningful opportunities for students to engage in self-assessment and peer feedback. The effect size for assessment-capable learners is 1.44, which indicates a profoundly positive impact.[4] When students understand the learning intentions and success criteria—and can evaluate their own progress—the potential learning gain can exceed three years' worth of academic growth.

Embed Essential Life Skills

Social-emotional competencies are not just "soft skills." They are essential life skills that support academic and personal success. According to the Collaborative for Academic, Social, and Emotional Learning (CASEL), these competencies should not be taught as isolated lessons or stand-alone programs, but rather embedded into everyday instruction and classroom culture. The intentional integration of academic standards and social-emotional competencies provides students with real-world scenarios to learn and practice their skills as they engage with more connected content.

Furthermore, by including school counselors in academic planning conversations, teams can more effectively integrate social-emotional learning competencies with academic learning goals.[5] School counselors bring valuable expertise in child development and social-emotional learning, and their perspective helps ensure that instruction supports the whole child academically, socially, and emotionally.

When considering the benefits of cross-disciplinary planning and teaching, it is hard to imagine doing anything different. Creating opportunities for student-centered instruction that makes content relevant, provides voice and choice, and embeds essential social-emotional competencies is a win for everyone. The next section of this chapter covers the steps to create cross-disciplinary units.

THE HOW

Conditions for successful cross-disciplinary planning and teaching include two crucial supports: time to plan and a clear process. This section starts with ways to find time for planning and then outlines the process that the CLT, or the interdisciplinary team, can use for cross-disciplinary planning.

Create Time for Cross-Disciplinary Planning

Cross-disciplinary planning and teaching is not new; unfortunately, the time required for collaboration across content areas and intentional planning often puts cross-disciplinary efforts last on the list. However, if time is organized thoughtfully and creatively, teachers can have the opportunity to engage in cross-disciplinary planning.

In the most ideal of schedules, teachers have time embedded in their day to engage in common planning, which could include cross-disciplinary planning. But when CLTs don't have this time, leaders must get creative about allotting time to engage in the work of cross-disciplinary planning. Remember that "it does not appear to be important until it is given time in the schedule."[6] If there is not regularly scheduled time in the CLTs day or week, leaders can explore the following options:

- Allocate professional development time to cross-disciplinary team planning meetings.
- Dedicate early release planning as time for teachers to collaborate.
- Take 15 minutes at the beginning of every staff meeting to allow disciplines to share what they are working on and find connections. If the staff meeting agenda can be emailed, then allocate the entire time to teacher collaboration.
- Arrange for substitute coverage. In an ideal world, this would be an entire day, but if this is not an option, consider partial-day substitutes who can cover 2 to 3 periods and allow multiple teams to meet for shorter periods.

> **PRO TIP**
> Create guiding questions to help students make better connections with the content they are learning in multiple areas.

Once teacher teams have been given time to plan for cross-disciplinary planning, the following steps provide the process.

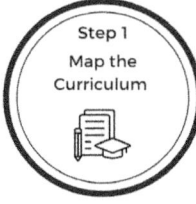

Map the Curriculum

To make cross-disciplinary planning easier, begin by outlining connected themes or topics in the team's content by month. This does not have to be a cumbersome process, but doing so creates a working timeline that guides the team's work in the following steps.

Connect Content

Connect broken down standards, identify crosscutting concepts, and embed social-emotional learning competencies. The goal is to identify crosscutting concepts and social-emotional learning competencies that can be woven together and addressed in multiple content areas.

To find these connections, teams can do the following:

- Choose themes or topics in common and connect them to unpacked Power Standards™ that you have already worked on in your CLT. (See Chapter 6 for more on breaking down standards.)
- Discuss how standards connect or cross over content areas.
- Identify crosscutting concepts and competencies that can be addressed in multiple classes and reinforced throughout the unit.
- Review the crosscutting concepts and find the interaction between content area and social-emotional learning competencies.
- Refine or create connected learning intentions.
- Discuss and plan for rigor. Be cognizant that social-emotional skills are continuously developing in students, and for some, building these skills can be the most rigorous part of learning. (See Chapter 5 for more on rigor.)

Assess

One of the most comprehensive ways to assess large cross-disciplinary units is through performance tasks. A performance task is an assessment where students are asked to apply their knowledge in a real-world context and can include a product or performance. In this step, teams create performance tasks that can be used across all content areas by using the learning intentions that include crosscutting concepts and embedded competencies.

Guidelines for creating performance tasks:

- Contribute to the assessment from the lens of the individual content grounded in the identified cross cutting concepts.
- Create the rubric as a team from the success criteria so that the rubric works for all content areas.
- Engage in collaborative scoring at the end of the assessment.

> **PRO TIP**
>
> During this step, individual teachers (via their CLT) may decide to create formative assessments to serve as checkpoints in their content areas. These data points can be discussed at team meetings to inform the unit and student progress. The team can also discuss opportunities for remediation and extension throughout the unit.

Reflect

As a team, take time to discuss what went well and what did not, making note of strategies, instructional moves, and assessment practices they may want to add, remove, or adjust in the future.

Sample reflection questions:

- What went well?
- What needs to be changed?
- What did our data show?
- What needs to be either added or removed? And why?

THE WHAT

This section includes a completed cross-disciplinary unit as an example to help your team use the planning template as they work through the steps in this chapter.

Sample 6th grade cross-disciplinary unit involving Reading and Writing, Math, Science, Social Studies, Music, and Art:

TEAM	AUGUST	SEPTEMBER	OCTOBER	NOVEMBER
1: ELA 2: SS 3: Math 4: Science 5: Music 6: Art	**Identity** *Who am I, and how do I belong in the world around me?*	**Community** *What does it mean to be a part of a community?*	**Change or Transformation** *How do things grow and change over time?*	**Systems and Structures** *What systems support life, learning, and societies?*

FEARLESS INSTRUCTION

THEME/TOPIC: IDENTITY	
Curricular Topics • Reading and Writing: Autobiographies, personal narratives, point of view • Math: Number sense review, ratios, graphing survey results • Science: Scientific method, introduction to ecosystems • Social Studies: Geography of Ohio and the US; civic responsibilities • Music: Music from diverse communities; rhythm and cultural identity • Art: Self-portraits, symbols of identity in art	**Crosscutting Concepts** • Identity • Community • Point of view • Data and interpretation • Interdependence • Reading, writing, interpreting, responding **Social-Emotional Competencies:** ❏ Self-Awareness ❏ Self-Management ❏ Responsible Decision-Making ❏ Relationship Skills ❏ Social Awareness

Connected Learning Intentions with Embedded Competencies:

- I am learning to use writing, visual art, and data so that I can express who I am. (Math, Art, Music, Social Awareness)
- I am learning to respectfully consider different points of view so that I can make better decisions. (Reading, Social Studies, Social Awareness & Responsible Decision-Making, Relationship Skills)
- I am learning to understand how authors, artists, and musicians share their perspectives so that I can explore and express my own ideas more clearly and creatively. (Reading, Music, Art, Social Awareness)
- I am learning to read graphs and charts so that I can better understand the world around me and use information to solve problems and make better decisions. (Math, Science, Decision-Making, Social Awareness)
- I am learning to explain how data helps us understand people and communities so that I can use evidence to make informed conclusions and better respond to the needs of others. (Social Studies, Math, Decision-Making)

Performance Task: *This Is Us*

Students create and share a multimedia profile that tells the story of who they are, where they come from, and how they see the world. They explore their identity, reflect on their role in the community, and consider how data and perspective shape the way they understand one another. Blending reading, writing, research, and creative expression, students connect what they're learning to who they are. Once all projects are completed, students come together in a class-wide showcase called "This Is Us."

> **Reflection**
> - *The Identity unit gave our students a meaningful way to connect who they are with what they're learning, and it showed. They were engaged, especially with their narratives and self-portraits, and the final showcase was a powerful reminder of what students can do when the learning is personal.*
> - *As a team, we were able to make strong cross-content connections, though we did notice some students needed more support in interpreting their data and staying on track with pacing.*
> - *Their reflections showed growth in confidence, relationships, and voice, and our academic data confirmed that while students could collect information, they needed more guidance drawing conclusions from it.*
> - *Next time, we'll build in more time for peer feedback, offer digital storytelling as a creative option, and adjust the science component so it fits more naturally with our themes of identity and interdependence.*

Visit the CASEL website for full definitions and resources on the social and emotional competencies.

ACTION STEPS

- ❏ Provide dedicated collaboration time for teachers to design, align, and reflect on cross-disciplinary units.
- ❏ Recognize completed units and highlight student learning outcomes through staff meetings, newsletters, or faculty shout-outs.
- ❏ Organize schoolwide events that showcase integrated learning.
- ❏ Use social media to share photos, student quotes, or highlights from the unit to demonstrate real-world relevance and community engagement.
- ❏ Invite local organizations, families, or experts into the learning experience to expand the reach and relevance of the work.
- ❏ Publicly recognize the time, collaboration, and creativity it takes to design meaningful cross-disciplinary instruction. This validation encourages others to participate and innovate.

Cross-Disciplinary Planning Template

Team Members	August	September	October	November	December

Team Members	January	February	March	April	May

Theme/Topic:

Curricular Topics:

Crosscutting Concepts:

Social-Emotional Competencies:
- ☐ Self-Awareness
- ☐ Self-Management
- ☐ Responsible Decision-Making
- ☐ Relationship Skills
- ☐ Social Awareness

Connected Learning Intentions with Embedded Competencies:

Performance Task:

Reflection:

2025 Creative Leadership Press. This page may be reproduced for classroom use only. All other rights reserved.

BIG IDEAS
RELATIONSHIPS
PRODUCTIVE STRUGGLE
HIGH EXPECTATIONS

OPEN YOUR HEART, CLEAR YOUR HEAD, FLEX YOUR HAND
Engage Everyone

WITH THIS FINAL PIECE, THE PICTURE IS COMPLETE—A reminder that every instructional decision matters. This chapter connects the strategies we have presented in this book to the heart of the matter: our students. This chapter focuses on the mindset of building relationships and connecting culturally to break through the barriers that keep students from learning.

> "When You Know Better, You Do Better"
> —MAYA ANGELOU

Our students come from different backgrounds, and they all have their own stories. Just as we expect our doctors to address a medical issue from our specific medical history, we must approach teaching and learning from an angle best suited for the one for which it is designed.

We know that the achievement gap largely stems from educators' inability to adapt to their students' needs. Douglas Reeves describes the courage to truly connect with our students and change the narrative as being "fearless." It's not a matter of teachers lacking the will—they genuinely want to help their students succeed. Rather, educators and leaders often lack the necessary knowledge and skills to guide students toward successful outcomes. But when teachers know better, they do better.

The end of this chapter includes an educator self-assessment that will provide you with insight and a path to ensure that your classroom is inviting and inclusive.

THE WHY

"Can You Teach Me To Read?"

As I entered Lanier High School in Jackson, Mississippi, the weight of its history and the legacy of its alumni struck me. Great leaders had once walked these halls, and there was a deep sense of pride associated with the Bulldog name. Now, it was my turn to shape the next generation of scholars and leaders within this community. The responsibility was immense.

Lanier was hosting a summer school program called "The 21st Century Computer Lab," where students learned about computers and various digital platforms. As I stepped into the classroom, a young student immediately recognized me. He stood up with excitement and approached me, saying, "Hi, my name is Cody. Are you the new superintendent?" His confidence in addressing the district's new leader was impressive. I shook his hand and confirmed his guess.

Then Cody asked a question that would shape my approach as the district's lead educator: "Will you teach me to read?" In that moment, I realized this was about more than just reading. It was about meeting Cody where he was and helping him connect the dots between what he knew and what he needed to learn.

As we consider our students, we do well to walk a mile in their shoes while also understanding that the pair of shoes they are in may be the only pair they have. Despite our good intentions, we sometimes lack a deep understanding of who they are, where they come from, or what drives them.

As we reflect further, we realize that we don't truly know how to reach them or engage them effectively enough to help them. We aspire to do better but are uncertain about how to proceed. Dr. Gary Howard aptly captures this in the provocative titles of his books *We Can't Teach What We Don't Know* and *We Can't Lead Where We Won't Go.*

> When I tried to understand Cody, I reflected on my own childhood. As an elementary student from a low-income neighborhood, I rode the bus to school, even though it wasn't far, because transportation was provided. I also relied on free lunch due to my socioeconomic status, but despite this, we didn't feel poor. My mother would say, "Just because you don't live in a mansion, doesn't mean you have to live like you live in a shack." I wondered if Cody had the same experiences and, if so, were there people in his life who helped him understand the context in which he lived.
>
> How did Cody live? How did he get to school? Was he able to take advantage of free lunch? Did he live with his parents? Did he have any siblings with which he had to share a bathroom or a homework desk?

We all have our own Cody—students we teach, lead, or mentor—who deserve adult advocates who make them feel a strong sense of belonging, a value to be carried from the community into the school. By fostering meaningful relationships, we can see and truly know our students, breaking through the barriers that hinder learning.

As we consider knowing who we teach, we must reflect on where our students live, how they interact with their peers and families outside of school, and what their hopes, dreams, wishes, and thoughts are about themselves and others. This insight allows us to make intentional instructional decisions and create a fearless environment that validates their experiences and supports their growth. When we deeply know our students, we are empowered to improve their outcomes.

Understanding the culture of our students is imperative to guiding them through a successful school year, as culture is how they make sense of the world. When we honor and reflect their cultural experiences in our classrooms, we create spaces where learning is rigorous, students are empowered, and they grow through challenge. In the next section, we'll explore practical ways to bring this mindset to life in every classroom.

> "Cultural values and learning practices transmitted from our parents and community guide how the brain wires itself to process information and handle relationships. Neural pathways are overdeveloped around one's cultural ways of learning."
>
> —ZARETTA HAMMOND, *CULTURALLY RESPONSIVE TEACHING & THE BRAIN*

THE HOW

There's an old saying that actions speak louder than words. This is the essence of a cultural mindset. Teachers communicate powerful messages, both intentionally and unintentionally, through their instructional choices. When educators skip standards or activities out of a belief that their students "can't," it sends a limiting message rooted in a deficit mindset. Instead, when educators focus on what students *can* achieve—with the right support—they build a culture of possibility. This belief comes to life when we anchor our practices in our values, promote rigor, set high expectations, and embrace productive struggle as a pathway to learning.

Anchor Actions in Values

Best-selling author Patrick Lencioni emphasizes that values are the foundational anchor of any organization. In a recent podcast episode titled "Aligning Values with Actions,"[1] Lencioni explains that values are not pulled out of thin air but are developed through the behaviors of the people of the organization. Lencioni shares an example of a team claiming integrity as a core value while engaging in borderline unethical behavior, illustrating a common gap between stated values and actual practices. He notes, "We do what we value, and we value what we do." To identify true core values, educators can apply Lencioni's perspective by observing the consistent behaviors of those who naturally and authentically reflect the school's ideals and contrasting them with those who inconsistently or unauthentically do so.

In our classrooms, we demonstrate our values by how we teach. Every moment is an opportunity to show students that they matter and that we believe in their brilliance. When we move beyond simply preparing students for a test, we open doors to creativity, critical thinking, and meaningful exploration. But when we continue to use the same lesson plans we have had for the last 20 years, we fail to address the innovation that instruction requires to reach the students of today. And when we extend our best efforts to every learner—not just those who are already succeeding—we live the belief that every student is capable, every student is worthy. If we are truly sincere about reaching our students, then we must connect the *who we teach* to the *how we teach*. Every student is worthy of the best instruction we can provide.

Create a Theory of Action

To build a culturally responsive mindset and foster holistic engagement, educators should ground their work in strategies that reach the Head (strategic thinking), the Heart (emotional connection), and the Hand (action and execution).[2] This process requires intentional planning and a clear commitment to core values and begins with creating a theory of action rooted in your values and what matters most for student learning.

> Strategies to create a theory of action:
> - Identify the instructional beliefs and core values that guide how you teach and how students experience learning in your classroom.
> - Design systems to gather meaningful feedback from students and use that input to adapt your instruction in ways that reflect those values and meet evolving student needs.

- Develop your own professional learning plan that reflects your values. Create a timeline for growth and reflection to hold yourself accountable.

When educators lead with values that are supported by strategy and action, every instructional decision becomes more intentional and more impactful.

Promote Rigor

Let's be clear. Rigor is not about working harder; it's about thinking deeper. Rigor does not mean more adding five more problems to the assignment or three more questions to the tests. Rigor does not just ask for an answer but requires reflection, analysis, and expression. True rigor asks students to own their learning, not just rent it for the test. It pushes past compliance into commitment.

Want to make rigor real? Include more purpose, more engagement, and more intellectual lift. Rigor isn't reserved for gifted classes or the "top kids." Rigor belongs to every child in every chair, every day. It says, "You deserve to wrestle with big ideas because you are capable of big thinking."

Strategies to promote rigor:

- Use performance tasks that mimic real-world challenges and require critical thinking across content areas.
- Facilitate fearless classroom discussions.[3]
  - Encourage divergent thinking and evidence-based arguments.
  - Set the roles for each group member.
  - Provide check-ins with the teacher during planning and check points before presentation.
  - Provide emotional and language support for students whom English is not their primary language.
- Encourage peer collaboration.[4]
  - Not as a structure for agreement but to work together to provide two or more alternative decisions.
  - Require them to include advantages and disadvantages that are thought-through and discussed.

When you know better, you know that rigor is respect, rigor is equity, rigor makes a statement. Rigor says, "I see what's in you, and I am going to help you pull it out of you." We don't increase rigor to break students down; we increase it to build them up, to stretch their minds, and to stir their souls. Rigor brings out the best in our students. If Cody had been gifted with rigor during learning in his earlier years, he would have been able to say, "Can I teach *you* to read?"

Empower Students Through High Expectations

When a teacher walks into a classroom with high expectations, they're not just setting a tone, they are singing a song. When teachers understand the how, the tune from their students changes from a single hum to a full choir. Students can feel when a teacher expects greatness and respond accordingly. High expectations say, "I believe in you enough to challenge you and empower you with your own learning." That belief becomes a mirror students hold up to themselves.

Educators model that every student is capable, worthy, and expected to grow: no exceptions, no excuses. For example, I remember Ms. Stansbury, my 10th-grade English teacher, never let her students opt out of thinking. When a student struggled in class, she would pull up a chair, look them in the eye, and say, "I know it's tough, but I also know you can do this. You've got it in you." She modeled error analysis and thinking aloud, and in doing so, showed students how to learn from mistakes instead of fearing them. Her room wasn't just a class; it was a fearless learning environment.

Move to Empowerment

Once a teacher has established high expectations for learning, the next step is to share ownership of those expectations and empower students to be cocreators.

Ideas for cocreating can be any of the following:

- Design the learning space together by encouraging students to share ideas for what should be in the room and what might hang on the walls.
- Invite students to craft their own classroom norms.
- Cocreate success criteria. Ask students questions such as these: What do you think this means? What do you think success would look like on this project?
- Give yourself permission to replace educational words with student words.
- Engage students in self-reported grades.

Encourage Productive Struggle

Real compassion does not mean easing the challenge. It means equipping students to meet it. When we encourage productive struggle, while elevating our instruction, we elevate belief in their brilliance.

Productive struggle, also known as wait time with a purpose, is another effective "how." This process encourages students to move from confusion to clarity. Struggle that's guided, encouraged, and celebrated becomes transformation.

Strategies to encourage productive struggle:

- Use Think-Alouds to model that messy process of grappling with a problem.
- Normalize "not knowing" as the first step to problem-solving.

- Use the persevere and return strategy. Avoid calling on another student to help or answer the question. Instead, provide the student with think time and return to them when they are ready to answer.

The "how" is not a mystery. It's a mindset. Hold expectations high, dig deep with rigor, and honor the struggle. Because when teachers *know better*, they *become better*. And when they become better, they light the path for every student to rise.

THE WHAT

Before we can lead students with clarity and conviction, we must first lead ourselves with honesty and intention. This self-assessment is not about perfection—it's about alignment. When our values guide our practice, our classrooms become places of purpose, connection, and growth.

As you reflect on the statements below, consider how your beliefs show up in your daily instruction, your relationships with students, and your own professional learning. Lean into this moment with courage and curiosity. Growth begins with knowing where you stand.

Fearless Instruction Educator Self-Assessment

1 – Not yet   **2** – Sometimes   **3** – Consistently

Anchor Action in Values

I can clearly articulate the instructional values and beliefs that guide my decisions and interactions with students.	1	2	3
I regularly seek feedback from students and use it to adjust my instruction based on how supported and challenged they feel.	1	2	3
I have identified specific areas for my professional growth that align with my values, and I remain committed to refining my practice in service of student success.	1	2	3

Promote Rigor

I assign work that requires students to think critically, not just recall facts.	1	2	3
I use real-world tasks and complex problems that stretch students' understanding.	1	2	3
I provide scaffolding, not shortcuts, and support without lowering the standard.	1	2	3

Empower Students Through High Expectations

I communicate to every student I encounter that I believe in their potential.	1	2	3
I plan lessons that reflect my belief in students' ability to reach grade-level standards.	1	2	3
I hold all students to high expectations, especially those who've been underestimated.	1	2	3

Encourage Productive Struggle

I encourage students to stay in the discomfort of learning without rushing to rescue them.	1	2	3
I acknowledge and celebrate mistakes as part of the learning journey.	1	2	3
I use strategies (e.g., Think-Alouds, peer collaboration) that promote perseverance.	1	2	3

Scoring Insights

- **30–36** You're building brilliance! Keep walking tall and reaching wide.
- **23–29** Solid ground. A few tweaks could turn good into transformational.
- **14–22** Time to recalibrate and refuel; your students need the best of you.
- **↓14** Be encouraged. This is the start of something better. Growth begins with honesty.

2025 Creative Leadership Press. This page may be reproduced for classroom use only. All other rights reserved.

ACTION STEPS

- **Reflect on Your "Why"**
  When things seem difficult, reconnect with your purpose as an educator.

- **Know Who You're Teaching**
  Take time to learn about your students' contexts, backgrounds, interests, and identities. Use that knowledge to build lessons that feel relevant and affirming.

- **Use Strategies That Engage Diverse Learners**
  Incorporate teaching strategies that reach students with different learning needs.

- **Design with EVERYONE in Mind**
  Evaluate your lesson plans and assessments: Are they accessible? Are they fair? Do they offer multiple ways for students to show what they know?

- **Align Values with Practice**
  Make sure your instructional choices reflect what you believe about your students' potential. High expectations paired with high support = empowerment.

- **Celebrate Progress, Not Perfection**
  Progress in student-centered teaching is ongoing. Celebrate small wins—one relationship, one lesson, one breakthrough at a time.

SECTION III REVIEW

Throughout this section, we explored how we reach all students through literacy, cross-disciplinary learning, and embracing the cultural mindset for instruction.

- In Chapter 9, we explored the importance of shared responsibility in making literacy a team sport. In this chapter, we drew a distinction between learning to read and reading to learn, recognizing that students, regardless of age or grade, can be anywhere along this continuum. We also reviewed high-leverage strategies that **all** teachers can use to foster literacy and vocabulary development across content areas.

- In Chapter 10, we applied what we learned about learning intentions and success criteria to interdisciplinary learning, while also embedding social-emotional learning competencies into academic content standards. This powerful framework fosters relevance by connecting content areas and motivates students through real-life learning scenarios.

- In Chapter 11, we explored how values and beliefs affect how we interact with students and the imperative to adopt the cultural mindset. Knowing our students is how we access them, but what we message is equally as important. When educators hold themselves and their students to high expectations, the sky is the limit.

REFLECTION QUESTIONS

- Does your school have a robust collection of multi-level, highly engaging texts for the curriculum? Does the collection include multimedia (podcasts, films, TED Talks, webinars) as well as texts from multiple perspectives?

- Does the daily schedule and annual calendar provide systematic times for teachers to share instructional practices, student achievement results, and plan together?

- If you were to prioritize your own learning, would you prefer it to be connected or siloed?

- How do personal experiences and background influence the way you connect with and understand students?

- How does my teaching (or leading) style reflect belief in students' potential?

FINAL THOUGHTS

NOW THAT WE HAVE EXAMINED AND THOUGHTFULLY ADDED ALL THE PIECES OF fearless instruction, let's take a step back and look at the full picture. Each chapter has offered more than just an instructional strategy; it has provided an important component of a larger, much more complex puzzle. From collaborative learning teams to data-informed decisions and from literacy as a framing force to rigor and clarity, each element has sharpened our understanding of what powerful and purposeful instruction looks like in our schools and classrooms. These aren't isolated strategies, and when implemented alone, they are less powerful than when they are brought together. Each element links to the next, deepening our understanding of the connection between teaching and learning.

The strategies shared within this book are intended to connect what can feel fragmented, to bring focus to practices and strategies that need clarity, and to create meaningful connections to the decisions we make in classrooms. Whether through feedback, nonfiction writing, or instructional leadership, each of these pieces plays a critical role in aligning our instructional efforts with the goal we all share: student success.

In the end, the impact of this work lies not in any single piece, but in how they all fit together with evidence, passion, and results. When we put our puzzle together with care, we create a complete and fearless picture of learning that includes every student, every voice, and every possibility.

ENDNOTES

Foreword

1. Hattie, John. *Visible Learning: The Sequel: A Synthesis of Over 2,100 Meta-Analyses Relating to Achievement*. Routledge, 2023.
2. Reeves, Douglas. *Achieving Equity and Excellence: Immediate Results from the Lessons Of High-Poverty, High-Success Schools*. Solution Tree Press, 2020.
3. Hattie, John. *Visible Learning for Teachers: Maximizing Impact on Learning*. Routledge, 2012.

Introduction

1. Chenoweth, Karin. *Schools That Succeed: How Educators Marshal the Power of Systems for Improvement*. Harvard Education Press, 2017.
2. Hattie, John. *Visible Learning: The Sequel: A Synthesis of Over 2,100 Meta-Analyses Relating to Achievement*. Routledge, 2023.
3. Hattie, John. *Visible Learning for Teachers: Maximizing Impact on Learning*. Routledge, 2012.

Chapter 1

1. Grissom, Jason A., Anna J. Egolite, and Constance A. Lindsay. "How Principals Affect Students and Schools: A Systematic Synthesis of Two Decades of Research." The Wallace Foundation, 2021. Available at http://www.wallacefoundation.org/ principalsynthesis.
2. Reeves, Douglas. *Fearless Schools: Building Trust, Resilience, and Psychological Safety*. Creative Leadership Press, 2023.
3. Reeves, Douglas. *Fearless Grading: How to Improve Achievement, Discipline, and Culture Through Accurate and Fair Grading*. Creative Leadership Press, 2023.
4. Reeves, Douglas. *Fearless Schools: Building Trust, Resilience, and Psychological Safety*. Creative Leadership Press, 2023.
5. Gajda, Rebecca, and Christopher J. Koliba. "Evaluating and Improving the Quality of Teacher Collaboration: A Field-Tested Framework for Secondary School Leaders." *NASSP Bulletin* 92, no. 2 (2008): 92. Sage Publications.

6   Hattie, John. *Visible Learning: The Sequel: A Synthesis of Over 2,100 Meta-Analyses Relating to Achievement*. Routledge, 2023.

7   Reeves, Douglas. *Fearless Classrooms: Building Resilience and Psychological Safety for Students, Staff, and Communities*. Creative Leadership Press, 2024.

Chapter 2

1   Shand, Robert, and Roger D. Goddard. "The Relationship Between Teacher Collaboration and Instructional Practices, Instructional Climate, and Social Relations." *Educational Policy* (2024): 1–26. Sage Publications. Accessed September 19, 2024.

2   DuFour, Rick, and Douglas Reeves. "The Futility of PLC Lite." *Phi Delta Kappan* 97, no. 6 (March 2016): 69–71.

3   Hattie, John. *Visible Learning: The Sequel: A Synthesis of Over 2,100 Meta-Analyses Relating to Achievement*. Routledge, 2023.

4   Ibid.

5   Boudett, Kathryn Parker, and Meghan Lockwood. "The Power of Team Norms." *Educational Leadership* 76, no. 9 (2019): 1–17. Accessed January 9, 2025.

6   Reeves, Douglas, and Robert Eaker. *100-Day Leaders: Turning Short-Term Wins Into Long-Term Success in Schools*. Solution Tree Press, 2019.

Chapter 3

1   DuFour, Rick, and Douglas Reeves. "The Futility of PLC Lite." *Phi Delta Kappan* 97, no. 6 (March 2016): 69–71.

2   Reeves, Douglas. *Fearless Classrooms: Building Resilience and Psychological Safety for Students, Staff, and Communities*. Creative Leadership Press, 2024.

3   Hammond, Zaretta. *Culturally Responsive Teaching and the Brain: Promoting Authentic Engagement and Rigor Among Culturally and Linguistically Diverse Students*. Corwin, 2015.

4   Stiggins, Rick. *The Perfect Assessment System*. ASCD, 2017.

Chapter 4

1   Reeves, Douglas. *Achieving Equity and Excellence: Immediate Results from the Lessons Of High-Poverty, High-Success Schools*. Solution Tree Press, 2020.

Chapter 5

1   Hattie, John, and Gregory M. Donoghue. "Learning Strategies: A Synthesis and Conceptual Model." *NPJ Science of Learning*, 1, no. 1 (2016). https://doi.org/10.1038/npjscilearn.2016.13.

2   Hess, Karen. *Rigor by Design, Not Chance: Deeper Thinking Through Actionable Instruction and Assessment*. ASCD, 2023.

3   Anderson, Lorin. W., and David R. Krathwohl. *A Taxonomy for Learning, Teaching and Assessing: A Revision of Bloom's Taxonomy of Educational Objectives*. Longman, 2001.

4   Webb, Norman L. Criteria for Alignment of Expectations and Assessments in Mathematics and Science Education. Council of Chief State School Officers and National Institute for Mathematics Education, Research Monograph No. 6. University of Wisconsin Center for Education Research, 1997.

5 Reeves, Douglas. *Fearless Grading: How to Improve Achievement, Discipline, and Culture Through Accurate and Fair Grading*. Creative Leadership Press, 2023.

Chapter 6

1 Hattie, John. *Visible Learning: The Sequel: A Synthesis of Over 2,100 Meta-Analyses Relating to Achievement*. Routledge, 2023.
2 Almarode, John, and Kara Vandas. *Clarity for Learning: Five Essential Practices That Empower Students and Teachers*. Corwin, 2018.
3 Reeves, Douglas. *Fearless Grading: How to Improve Achievement, Discipline, and Culture Through Accurate and Fair Grading*. Creative Leadership Press, 2023.
4 Gonzalez, Jennifer. "Meet the Single-Point Rubric." *Cult of Pedagogy* (February 4, 2015). Accessed April 2, 2025. https://www.cultofpedagogy.com/single-point-rubric/.
5 Reeves, Douglas. *Fearless Schools: Building Trust, Resilience, and Psychological Safety*. Creative Leadership Press, 2023.

Chapter 7

1 Reeves, Douglas, and Robert Eaker. *100-Day Leaders: Turning Short-Term Wins Into Long-Term Success in Schools*. Solution Tree Press, 2019.
2 Reeves, Douglas. *Achieving Equity and Excellence: Immediate Results from the Lessons of High-Poverty, High-Success Schools*. Solution Tree Press, 2020.
3 Hattie, John. *Visible Learning: The Sequel: A Synthesis of Over 2,100 Meta-Analyses Relating to Achievement*. Routledge, 2023.
4 Reeves, Douglas. *Achieving Equity and Excellence: Immediate Results from the Lessons of High-Poverty, High-Success Schools*. Solution Tree Press, 2020.

Chapter 8

1 Reeves, Douglas. *Fast Grading: A Guide to Implementing Best Practices*. Solution Tree Press, 2016.
2 Ainsworth, Larry, and Jan Christinson. *Five Easy Steps to a Balanced Math Program for Upper Elementary Grades*. Advanced Learning Press, 2006.
3 Reeves, Douglas. *Fearless Schools: Building Trust, Resilience, and Psychological Safety*. Creative Leadership Press, 2023.
4 Hattie, John. *Visible Learning: A Synthesis of Over 800 Meta-Analyses Relating to Achievement*. Routledge, 2009.
5 Reeves, Douglas. *Fast Grading: A Guide to Implementing Best Practices*. Solution Tree Press, 2016.
6 Ibid.
7 Ibid.
8 John Hattie, discussion with Majalise Tolan, June 18, 2011.

Chapter 9

1. Anderson, Richard C., Paul T. Wilson, and Linda G. Fielding. "Growth in Reading and How Children Spend Their Time Outside of School." *Reading Research Quarterly* 23, no. 3 (1988):285–303.
2. Gough, Philip, and William E. Tunmer. "Decoding, Reading, and Reading Disability." *Remedial and Special Education* 7, no. 1 (1986):6–10.
3. Collins, Jim. *Good to Great: Why Some Companies Make the Leap and Others Don't*. Random House, 2001.
4. Hattie, John. *Visible Learning: The Sequel: A Synthesis of Over 2,100 Meta-Analyses Relating to Achievement*. Routledge, 2023.
5. Bear, Donald, Marcia Invernizzi, Shane Templeton, and Francine Johnston. *Words Their Way: Word Study for Phonics, Vocabulary, and Spelling Instruction*, 7th ed. Pearson, 2020. Beck, I. L., M. G. McKeown, and L. Kucan. *Creating Robust Vocabulary: Frequently Asked Questions and Extended Examples*. Guilford Press, 2008. Beck, I. L., M. G. McKeown, and L. Kucan. *Bringing Words to Life: Robust Vocabulary Instruction*. Guilford Press, 2013. Graves, M. F. *The Vocabulary Book: Learning and Instruction*. Teachers College Press, 2016.
6. Frayer, Dorothy Ann, Wayne C. Frederick, and Herbert John Klausmeier. *A Schema for Testing the Level of Cognitive Mastery: Report from the Project on Situational Variables and Efficiency of Concept Learning*. Wisconsin Research and Development Center for Cognitive Learning, 1969.
7. Bear, Donald, Marcia Invernizzi, Shane Templeton, and Francine Johnston. *Words Their Way: Word Study for Phonics, Vocabulary, and Spelling Instruction*, 7th ed. Pearson, 2020.

Chapter 10

1. Dewey, John. *The School and Society: Being three lectures by John Dewey supplemented by a statement of the University Elementary School*. University of Chicago Press, 1907.
2. Berckemeyer, Jack. *Successful Middle School Teaming*. Association for Middle Level Education, 2002.
3. Ibid.
4. Hattie, John. *Visible Learning: The Sequel: A Synthesis of Over 2,100 Meta-Analyses Relating to Achievement*. Routledge, 2023.
5. Perez, Ann McCarty, and Elise Kenney-Caldwell. *The Successful Middle School Counseling Program*. Association for Middle Level Education, 2023.
6. Perez, Ann McCarty. *The Successful Middle School Schedule*. Association for Middle Level Education, 2022.

Chapter 11

1. Lencioni, Patrick. "Values Are Verbs." At the Table with Patrick Lencioni. Episode 227 (May 2024). Accessed May 15, 2025. https://www.tablegroup.com/227-values-are-verbs/.
2. Gray, Cedrick. *The Successful Middle School Leader*. Association for Middle Level Education, 2023.
3. Reeves, Douglas. *Fearless Classrooms: Building Resilience and Psychological Safety for Students, Staff, and Communities*. Creative Leadership Press, 2024.
4. Reeves, Douglas. *Fearless Grading: How to Improve Achievement, Discipline, and Culture Through Accurate and Fair Grading*. Archway Publishing, 2023.

ABOUT THE AUTHORS

Allyson Apsey

Allyson Apsey, Director of Client Relations at Creative Leadership Solutions, brings her 25 years of experience to partner with schools and districts to deliver tailored, high-impact professional development. With experience as an award-winning principal at all levels, she brings firsthand expertise in effective leadership and instruction. Allyson is also a nationally recognized keynote speaker and bestselling author known for inspiring and empowering educators. On stage or in print, her voice resonates, helping educators feel seen, supported, and equipped to create meaningful change that positively impacts student learning.

Michelle Cleveland

Dr. Michelle Ellen Cleveland has served in public education since 2001 as a teacher, administrator, and district leader in San Bernardino City Unified. She is currently Director of Accountability and Educational Technology as well as a principal leadership coach. Michelle is also a facilitator for the NCEE leadership development program. She holds degrees from Scripps College (BA), Chapman University (MA), and San Diego State (EdD). In 2018, she was honored as a Scripps College Distinguished Alumna for her work in public education.

Terry Chevalier-Metzger

Dr. Terry Metzger has over 35 years experience in PK–12 education, serving as a teacher, principal and superintendent. In addition to teaching educational leadership at the university level, Terry coaches and mentors new and aspiring educational leaders throughout California. Her current work includes the development and implementation of fair and accurate grading practices, professional learning communities, pathways for post-secondary success, and authentic literacy practices.

ABOUT THE AUTHORS

Tony Flach

Tony Flach is a seasoned educator and leader with over 20 years of experience driving school improvement nationwide. A former teacher, coach, and administrator in Norfolk, VA, Tony is passionate about equity and student achievement through data-driven practices. He has held leadership roles in a Broad Prize-winning district, worked with educational publishers, and supported schools in launching and refining impactful initiatives. Grounded in classroom experience and committed to systemic change, Tony believes every school should be one he'd proudly send his own children to.

Emily Freeland

Dr. Emily Freeland brings over 32 years of experience in education, including leadership roles at the state, district, and school levels and teaching science. She has focused on underperforming schools, using data to drive improvement, close achievement gaps, and boost graduation rates. As an Instruction and Leadership Coach, she supports schools nationwide. Her book, *From Ghost to Graduates*, showcases her work as a certified National Dropout Prevention Specialist and offers strategies to reengage students, including those impacted by pandemic learning.

Cedrick Gray

Dr. Gray is a nationally recognized educator, former superintendent, and executive pastor whose leadership blends instructional excellence with deep cultural insight. With over two decades in education, he has fearlessly led schools and systems toward equity, belonging, and brilliance. Best known for his transformational work in middle schools, Dr. Gray equips educators to center student voice, challenge the status quo, and lead with both courage and compassion. His work reminds us that fearless instruction begins where belonging takes root—and where leaders are bold enough to believe in every child's brilliance.

Ann McCarty Perez

Dr. Ann Perez, Director of Professional Learning at Creative Leadership Solutions, has served for 28 years as a teacher, assistant principal, principal, executive director of teaching and learning, and now, coach. A graduate of Bowling Green State University, The Ohio State University, and Virginia Tech, Dr. Perez is passionate about developing adults to support student success. Her favorite strategy for change is the master schedule, believing anything is possible with a great schedule.

Michelle Picard

Dr. Michelle Picard is a passionate educator with over 30 years of experience leading transformational change in K–12 and university settings. She has served as a teacher, instructional coach, ELA Supervisor (K–12), and Director of Early Childhood and Elementary Education. Michelle holds a doctorate in reading and educational leadership from the University of Virginia. Her expertise includes literacy instruction, high-leverage strategies, curriculum design with diverse representation, assessment analysis, and practices that increase engagement and performance.

Melissa Stephanski

Dr. Melissa Stephanski is a passionate educator with over 27 years in K–12 education, serving as a teacher, counselor, alternative school lead, principal, and assistant superintendent in one of Kentucky's largest districts. Her experience spans urban, suburban, and rural settings. She holds a doctorate in Educational Leadership and multiple certifications in counseling and administration. As a coach and consultant, she presents nationally and internationally on leadership, PLCs, and school culture, with a focus on supporting new administrators and fostering environments where teaching and learning thrive.

Bill Sternberg

Dr. Bill Sternberg's 27-year tenure in education includes former roles as a special education teacher, elementary principal, state education project director, and school district assistant superintendent within urban, suburban and rural settings. Throughout his career, Bill has remained passionate about the focus on calibration of expectations for proficient student work within school environments through an analysis of learning standards as a means to reach ALL learners. In his current role, Bill works with teachers and leaders nationally as they seek to enhance their professional practice.

Majalise W. Tolan

Dr. Majalise Tolan has been a teacher, coach, and activity director and began her administrative career as a high school assistant principal and athletic director. She has also served as an intermediate principal, middle school principal, and high school principal. She was a secondary director prior to serving as the superintendent of a rural Oregon district. She co-authored *She Leads: The Women's Guide to a Career in Educational Leadership*. Majalise lives in Oregon with her husband, four kids, two dogs, and two cats, and she spends as much time as possible reading and walking on the beach.

Bring Creative Leadership Solutions to Your School or District

Creative Leadership Solutions is a leading provider of research and evidence-based professional development and coaching for K-12 education. We partner with districts and schools to achieve their goals, impact student learning, and improve performance. Our team of experts is dedicated to delivering personalized and differentiated learning opportunities.

Learn more at www.creativeleadership.net
Contact us at service@creativeleadership.net

www.ingramcontent.com/pod-product-compliance
Lightning Source LLC
Chambersburg PA
CBHW081200230426
43666CB00016B/2871